The Following Plough

The Use of Praying
Five for Sorrow, Ten for Joy
Friday Afternoon

J. NEVILLE WARD

The Following Plough

As the plough follows words, so God rewards prayers.
— WILLIAM BLAKE

This is a reprint of the edition published in Great Britain by
Epworth Press.

International Standard Book No.: 0-936384-18-2
Library of Congress Catalog No.: 84-71179

Published in the United States of America by Cowley
Publications.
Cover design by James Madden, SSJE

TO
Jonathan and Antonia

Contents

1 Journey in Faith   11

2 Recollection in Tranquillity   33

3 The Following Plough   49

4 On Dryness   63

5 Masculine, Feminine
and the Spiritual   85

6 Mother of God   103

I

Journey in Faith

I THOUGHT of using the word 'pilgrimage', but it seemed rather portentous. I have been a drifter rather than a pilgrim. A pilgrim generally has a goal of some kind, a shrine perhaps, even a grail. There has been nothing like that in my life to give a purpose to experience. Thinking about God is not something I have particularly wanted to do for its own sake. It has been stimulated mainly by the way life has stirred or disturbed my mind.

Everyone is religious in this sense. All react to experience with some form of love or enjoyment or fear or rage, except those driven to shelter from the ambiguous rain of life under some dreadful apathy. Religion concerns some attempt to sift and understand those reactions, organize them into a coherent attitude, arrange a readiness in oneself for more of the happier sort. It is not everyone who wants to do that, but all have the reactions, the stuff of religion.

I find it hard to think of God at all when I am miserable, very easy when I am happy. This is because when you are miserable you are usually disliking God intensely and you prefer not to look at him, just as when you are talking with someone you dislike you are unwilling to register the full reality of this person and address your remarks to a point about six inches to the left of his right ear.

Not thinking about God does not mean not knowing him. It simply means not naming him. Most people, indeed, in one sense, all people, know God, but many do not name him. It is just a matter of words and the willingness to identify a certain presence.

I am sure that I have been given faith, in the sense that I have never been interested in the question of God's existence. It has never been open to question for me. I was given a mind quite sure of that, just as I was given a mind that words sink in and numbers bounce off. Someone said of William Blake that for him 'the veil of outer things seemed always to tremble with some breath behind it . . . and the pulse of every minute sounded as the falling foot of God'. That is a rather lyrical way of putting it—indeed I think it was Swinburne who said it, but when I meet that range of ideas it is like coming into the light, into open country where you can breathe again.

God's nature, what he is in fact like, is another matter altogether; but certainty of his being was simply given to me and has never not been there. Of the three so-called 'theological' virtues, faith, hope and love, the other two are in a totally different world of experience. If they are gifts of God, as Christians are taught, they are nevertheless a peculiarly unreliable presence in most lives. My supply of them seems to run out every two days.

Since we are not consulted about what point in history and what place on the earth's surface we are pushed into life, the start of a spiritual journey is never something anyone does. It is, like life itself, something received from other people.

For what you have received you may be truly thankful; you may be perplexed by it, or so offended that some hidden resentment is always at its deep work of eating you hollow; but some sense of the givenness of life is one of those spiritual realizations that come fairly soon and tend to remain with you, part of the pleasant or threatening way the world looks at you.

Seven years at Kingswood, John Wesley's school, gave me the beginnings of sensitiveness to five realms—the value of reason, the goodness of the body, the pleasure and pain in personal relationships, the call to service, the appreciation of beauty. What more could one possibly want from education? We were surrounded by formal religion, of course. It was there all the time, but unobtrusively, rather like the ticking of a clock. It was more obvious in the clerical homes to which most of us returned for the holidays. At school we discussed it respectfully, perhaps a little apprehensively as though we felt the ground marshy under our feet and were frightened of being sucked in. I went up to Oxford preferring Plato to Jesus. I thought the one who bore the greater name insufficiently sensitive to the beautiful, and I was perplexed about his attitude to the Pharisees. I still think that the New Testament is an underdeveloped world aesthetically, and I shrink before the wind of anti-semitism that rather often blows through it.

In my last year at school, however, I had had a small spiritual disturbance. It came quite unexpectedly, though very vividly, so vividly that it is always associated in my memory with the actual place where it happened. I suddenly found myself, for no apparent reason, thinking of Jesus for the first time as an intriguing individual. At that moment the pietistic, sentimental Sunday School image of him that I had been hating for years dropped away for ever, and in its place was at last a man, a stranger certainly, but real and interesting.

That first response to him has never faded but it has become very complicated and elusive. If I sensed then a little of the quality *fascinosum* in Jesus, since then it has been his ambiguous relationship with the ultimate, with God's *mysterium tremendum*, that has tantalized me, so that I find words like 'intriguing' ridiculously out of place when applied to Jesus. I sometimes love what he seems to be and to represent, but sometimes I cannot bear him and often wish he had never said some of the things he is supposed to have said. But it is as difficult to hide from him as it is sometimes to look for him. There is an alarming vitality about the gospels that cannot be manipulated. You cannot dismiss any reported saying of Jesus, even if it is clearly anachronistic or of dubious historicity. Because it has been meditated, prayed over, suffered for, through all these perplexed centuries, it acquires some at any rate of the power of his name, as the supposed fragment of the true cross in a reliquary gathers a grace that is not disturbed by the demonstration of its inauthenticity. Any time some passage that has been dead for you for years may suddenly disturb your peace, or wipe out your sadness, no longer a harmless thing of straw but alive, like Petrushka in Stravinsky's ballet.

There is a hymn which Methodists sing that urges the eternal son, the eternal love, to take to himself his mighty power. For that to happen, room has to be made in the believer's mind. The word 'Christ' has to assume wider significances than a man, even the son of man, can sustain; otherwise his presence diminishes and recedes into the past. The eucharistic Christ is a concentration of meanings more universal than the particulars of Jesus given us in the Christian writings. What we know from those sources is filled out by what he has come to stand for, by an accumulation of reference and association that has grown in solemnity and radiance as in each new generation more people have brought his name into their lives. When we pray in the Eucharist that our food and drink may make us one body with him, 'him' is the love that pours from God ceaselessly into the world, misunderstood here, coming like the scent of spring there, at one time a loyalty, at another a daring, but always identified in the experience of individuals by the pain and infinite worth that seem to belong to love as blood to life.

This glorified Christ, transfigured so that you see Moses and Elijah with him (and Bach and Beethoven and Michelangelo and Blake and all the mighty ones of old) can take into himself and make creative the most radical treatment of the Jesus of history by critical investigation. Indeed he can own and use everything that stretches faith to the point of pain, like the ebb of the spirit in the organized Church, the loneliness of belief in this grim pit the twentieth century has become, and all the other ills that Christian flesh is heir to. He marvellously teaches one how to care and not to care. I would have lost interest long ago if all sorts of people had not helped me to see him.

My generation of theological students had to come to some sense of certainty about our vocation with minds much occupied by the imminence of the Second World War, its causes, the right and wrong of it. So during ministerial training and the first years of my ministry it was naturally the practical world of various ethical considerations that life thrust in my face. Some awarenesses, some attitudes reached then, relating to the interesting but complicated world of moral decision, remain part of my response to life still. Though I hardly ever turn to them now, I derived so much from Bergson's *Two Sources of Morality and Religion*, the writings of Reinhold Niebuhr, and the work of Nicolas Berdyaev that I think of them with great affection and gratitude even though I understand that Austin Farrer once referred to the work of Berdyaev as 'vaticinatory bosh'. I realize now that Berdyaev played moral theology with the sustaining pedal down all the time, but at that part of my journey he was a huge inspiration; and it was he who directed me to the novels of Dostoevsky, in whose atmosphere of *angst* and heady vision my mind reeled and my faith grew.

However, two other presences from that time have stayed with me, continually speaking and encouraging me to listen. The writings of Martin Buber, particularly *I and Thou*, *Between Man and Man*, and *Mamre*, have opened up to me the deep world of intimacy and understanding, what it means to be truly in relationship with another person, to be really present, without forfeiting or concealing any of your own reality yet allowing the other similarly to be really present to you in the fulness of his or her love and fear and need to grow. There are few more rewarding meditations than the theme of being open to oneself and to others in honesty and trust, allowing them the same freedom, and sympathetically encouraging its articulation but not pressurizing them into an honesty they are not yet able to sustain. It is in this way that human beings make progress towards that mutually unprotected warmth in which their innermost wants and fears are at last free to show their pale faces.

Buber's book *I and Thou* seemed to many people an intensely religious book. It is significant that the 'Thou' in the title referred initially to Buber's wife. The only religion worth spending time on is rooted in the way we negotiate day to day experience of people and events. It is in the undefensive openness to persons, to each day's experience, that people meet the abiding, numinous reality that is called the living God. It is there that he is found to be continually addressing them and waiting for each personal answer. We need to examine and describe this meeting, we want to do this, because it is by far the most exciting and important encounter given us to talk about, but the language of observation and statement has too large a mesh to gather it all, and some of it will always slip through. Martin Buber was very much alive to these sensitive considerations.

The other continuing presence has been the poetry of T. S Eliot. He wrote *The Waste Land* as an expression of a very 'complex tissue of feelings and desires', but rarely has a man's private predicament so vitally touched a public nerve. In that poem's obscurity and beauty, haunted as it is by so many voices of European and Eastern tradition, twentieth-century imaginations have continually recognized, with an odd kind of comfort, their own perplexity and hope. Particularly in its images of drought and thirst, our longing for faith, for God, for the water of grace to refresh the impoverished spiritual life of our time, finds itself acknowledged in a period when Christian worship is not brave or honest enough to acknowledge it. And its episodic character, its voices that speak from situations only briefly indicated, its persons caught for a moment in some context of unexpected meaning—these features themselves speak the loss of wholeness, the waiting for new unities and integrations, through which our difficult time lives.

Eliot's later *Four Quartets*, thought by many to be his supreme achievement, have certainly been more readily and gratefully accepted by Christians, perhaps particularly because as a set of variations on the theme of time and the timeless they assume much profound Christian attitude and conviction that is rarely heard in the ministry of the word and the conversation of believers in the local church. The absence of talk about it does not alter the fact that ordinary men and women do have moments of special perception (by means of light or sound or scent or memory) in which experience becomes transparent and they may wonder if they are seeing a little beyond the world of appearances. Eliot takes these moments, marvellously, and relates them to the experience of the mystic and to the blurred and prosaic character of much daily life, all the time bringing out things new and old from the huge store of Christian wisdom with a confidence and hope he had not reached in the earlier work. To read him is a civilizing exercise, it is also to meet catholic Christianity, and the two have much to do with each other though it is not so obvious today as it used to be.

Nowadays we inevitably see Eliot's later and earlier work as a whole, permeated by mutual influence. However, I am increasingly drawn to *The Waste Land*. Its images stay in the mind, ready to slip into other contexts.

> Then Jesus was led up by the Spirit into the wilderness to be tempted by the devil. And he fasted forty days and forty nights, and afterwards he was hungry. And the tempter came and said to him, 'If you are the Son of God, command these stones to become loaves of bread'. But he answered, 'It is written, "Man shall not live by bread alone, but by every word that proceeds from the mouth of God".'

In that fragment of the gospel poetry I now cannot help seeing a man, in the waste land of his time, any time, our time, arguing with himself the question 'what do men live by, what is there for them to live by, what gives life?' And then the passage blends, powerfully, with another:

> What are the roots that clutch, what branches grow
> Out of this stony rubbish? Son of man,

You cannot say, or guess, for you know only
A heap of broken images, where the sun beats,
And the dead tree gives no shelter, the cricket no relief,
And the dry stone no sound of water.[1]

When I began the journey of faith I never dreamed how important a place reading was going to have in it, that it would be quite simply the principal form of the ministry of the word in the Christian life. However, there are so many different kinds of people who want God, that recommending books to feed that want is a very hit and miss affair. It is never easy to achieve spiritual empathy with someone whom Christ is calling along a route that is strange to you. Suppose you are at the time of life when the search for meaning is assuming increasing importance, and the desire for the feeling of continuity, for the assurance that, given the way time consigns experience to the past, the past is something more vital and abiding than a waste-paper basket. That brand of ache almost disqualifies you for some important sympathies with people who are at a different stage of the route. There is also the dullness that plagues organized religion. As you grow older you become harder to please, you find it a rarer experience to come across something that touches the right spot and sets up that pain of wanting God which shows you that the old nerve is still trembling there, not yet dead. Books that do anything for me must give me a sharper vision of the world, a fresh awareness of the way faith makes sense of it, and replenish the sense of its mystery. I am most helped by books that are not too committed, not afraid to be uncertain, have ambiguities that make you want to look again (like well-made music in which you never hear everything at first encounter)

[1] T. S. Eliot, *The Waste Land: The Complete Poems and Plays of T. S. Eliot*, Faber and Faber 1969, p. 61

and, especially, go on working in the mind, even if at times inopportunely.

There is one conviction that has deepened steadily, to become a river of meaning that has certainly helped faith to grow and spread. It is the certainty of the Holy Spirit's presence in the dialectical and dynamic character of life, the realization that tension and conflict, statement and counterstatement, are the stones in the road we walk to the knowledge of God's will or the knowledge of what we think God's will may be. In few situations can the question be asked in the form 'who is right? who has the truth?' None is right, none has the truth in any absolute sense. Every good arrangement is destined (and this is not a doom) to prove unsatisfactory and to require correction. The hunger to be right, to win the argument, is a longing for forbidden fruit that rises from anxiety. So is the desire for theological neatness and definition. Anything that we say about God must always be somewhere, in some sense, not true, because it requires extension and modification by what must also be said about him. It is good for Christians to do what can be done together, bearing with tension and difference, making our temporary clearings, in faith that God is at work too and will give what we do or suffer such meaning as it can bear.

I came to see that one's spiritual life would increasingly involve coming to terms with this abandonment of absolutism and perfectionism. I could see its wisdom clearly but was very reluctant to practise it, my involuntary imagination being so cluttered with idealized images of life, of other people and not least of myself. I now think that to be united with Christ is to be making progress in seeing life as it is, not as the child within you wishes it to be, and receiving grace to love its real presence. When reality is mystifying, love will accept being mystified. The poet Keats' idea of 'negative capability', the state of mind of one who is 'capable of being in uncertainties, mysteries and doubts, without any irritable reaching after fact and reason . . . remaining content with half knowledge',[2] not wanting to have it all clear, not playing God and continually re-making the world in one's own image, is a useful statement of this feature of journeying in faith.

It took me, emerging from a theological college, about five years to think I had found my feet in the work of a minister. I felt free enough then to notice what most interested me in it. These assessments are always a mixture of genuine observation and projection of personal need, but it was clear to me that one set of questions nagged in the mind like toothache: what it means to know God, how the Christian tradition understands this, the different ways in which different personalities experience him, the superficialities and illusions and despairs you can fall into when you want God, what you could expect to happen in your life if you gave God a trial run, say, for about a year. I wanted to know this for myself, I saw that others certainly did, though they rarely said so (there's surprisingly little talk about God in the local church), and I certainly felt that though there were many topics on which a minister might be forgiven for seeming a fool he ought not to cut such a sad figure on this subject. By a marvellous grace I was led to the literature of prayer, and at the same time I began trying to learn how to be still in God's presence.

In the extensive literature of prayer two books have had and still have a place in the centre of my thankfulness. One is the anonymous *The Cloud of Unknowing*, and the other is J. P. de Caussade's *Abandonment to Divine Providence*. The teaching of de Caussade immediately

[2] *Letters of John Keats*, ed. Frederick Page, Oxford University Press 1965, p. 53

spoke to my condition, particularly his way of negotiating the ceaseless drive and complexity of time by reducing them to what he calls the sacrament of the present moment. The idea is itself part of his equally practical and commonsense view of the will of God as a two-fold permitting and willing things to happen. The whole setting of a believer's life at any given moment, including his pains and fears and the accumulated agony of the world, is to be seen as permitted by God, since all that is in fact what is happening now. On the other hand, the active will of God is what he wishes the believer consciously and deliberately to do in this moment, and it always involves his attending to the duty or bearing the pain or enjoying the pleasure which life is immediately presenting to him.

To accustom yourself to the presence of God and learn how to live with such a tremendous name, so near and yet so strange, is something that obviously goes on in the mind. It has to do with how we treat our minds and how they treat us.

Most people seem to sense that life is a fragmentary affair and rather disillusioning, that it tends to get out of control and yet again and again succeeds in shaping up into happiness for a while, and that it's always worth while hoping that it will manage this trick for you. This is where the people are, this is where they live mostly, in their loves and wants and the attendant shadow of dread these always trail. At a more reflective level there is their alternating feeling of freedom and helplessness, their suspicion that if you look too hard for the point of your existence it vanishes, their surprise that so much that is happening in the world, as it is brought to their notice in the news each night, is so unpleasant. The life of faith is a matter of understanding all this mental material in terms of the will of God and trying to organize it accordingly.

Of all the contents of the mind that resist the religious organization and understanding of one's life none are so strong as our resentments and fears. I saw this to be true of myself, and my pastoral work soon convinced me it was true of everyone else. The people who wanted help from me certainly wanted help in knowing God but it was obvious that their spiritual difficulties were all in some way connected painfully with their angers and dreads.

So I wanted very much to understand this darkness of resentment and fear in which so much of life is lived. I soon found that that subject, the inner world of people's emotional life, has a remarkable amount to do with spirituality. Indeed the two studies became and have remained my principal interests. They have often seemed to be one and the same thing. To follow, in a case history, the sensitive, unhurried persistence of an analyst helping a confused and frightened human being to self-understanding and fresh interest in his struggle for growth is to be given incidentally an image of the compassion of Christ.

A priest has the peculiar joy and embarrassment of being so involved in the complicated and sensitive thing he is doing that it is a question who is pastor and who are flock. Indeed that antique rural metaphor is just about played out. You are not a 'have' confronting a bunch of 'have-nots', not a dispenser of something they want (at any rate in the only dimension of the life of the Church that matters); you and they (and the lapsed, the hostile, the despairing who never come near) are all wanters. You stand with them in the mystery of existence with its fragmentary perceptions of something more human, more natural than this, and you want the grace of things and the resolution of the daily contradictions as much as they do.

I soon became rather impressed with the discovery how lonely and unhelped a minister is. Something of huge importance was missing. I needed someone with whom to assess the situation from time to time, to discuss the spiritual reluctances, evasions, misunderstandings that clutter the route to God. At the same time, the ability to sympathize (of which no one ever has enough) would obviously be extended and deepened if I myself was regularly at the receiving end of a relationship in which spiritual counsel is given.

I wanted that good thing in a sacramental context. A friend introduced me to an Anglican monk who very kindly agreed to act as spiritual director though he characteristically shrank from the name as being paternalist. He helped me to understand and accept the grace of the sacrament of penance. And through the years the renewal and encouragement I have been given in this way, with a number of directors of great patience and affection, form a considerable part of what I understand as the mercy of Christ.

Incidentally, for some time now most people have observed with dismay the extraordinary decline in the power of preaching, both in the skill of the preachers and in the Christian congregation's expectation of grace from this ministry. It is worth noting that in sacramental confession the ministry of the word still retains its power. Why it should do so is in part inherent in the circumstances. It is addressed to someone who wants it and has deliberately come for it, who has honestly tried as well as he can to say how it is with him and believes that what he now hears will be God's word for his situation. And it is offered by someone who has listened first, has tried to understand, and now speaks, heart to heart, affectionately, with the one desire to help his brother understand himself and find his freedom in Christ.

I have found religion an experience remarkably un-illuminated by dramatic moments of memorable grace. I see the growth of conviction in the life of faith as pro-tracted, slow, often seeming to come to a standstill, rather like an incoming tide, one wave after another pushing forward and dying in an ineffectual spread of foam, but coming a little further up the beach with each persevering effort. So that there has to be trust. The more trust there is, and the less struggle, the better the life of faith goes. And gradually the sense of receiving, of being given this and that, comes.

That relaxed thing, the sense that life is a giver, that there is no need to compete or perform, is charac-teristically Christian, part of the Jesus life-style. The main channels of it in my experience have been the Eucharist, music, poetry, silence, and being admitted deeply into people's lives.

When I came into the work of the ministry the Euchar-ist was a dead routine. About nine years later I began teaching and preaching a sacramental Christianity with a conviction and joy that amounted to a release. This development had something to do with my discovering Gregory Dix's *The Shape of the Liturgy*, the work of Eugene Masure, and also with the inherent chanciness of the spiritual life. It is often the case that one is ready for a new perception and cannot explain why this should be so. Mysteriously a moment of truth had come, a door had opened in my mind, and (it seems to me now) Christ-ianity walked in and poured its infinite store in front of me, so that I wondered what I had been living with before. I now saw the Eucharist as the solemn and beauti-ful concentration of all the Christian meanings that makes it the beating heart of the Church. This view of worship has remained and become so absorbing that I have to admit that the other forms of worship we go in for seem to me rather thin and uninteresting things.

There is praise in many lives, a kind of worship, whenever people respond joyfully, gratefully, generously to existence. The reason for the Christian group's coming together in its specially articulate worship is to give thanks for Christ, and to renew the offering of their lives to him and their acceptance of all that he means. In this way the Eucharist brings together and identifies its miscellaneous crowd who most of the time are just a number of individuals submerged in the ocean of humanity. At the same time it focuses the faith of all (of whatever religion or none) who think they detect in their own wanting an inner hunger and thirst, who suspect that through the dark drift of appearances a love beyond this world is asking to be turned into body and blood.

It is a way of saying 'Look, human life is essentially and continually need!' All the packed complexity of men's and women's experience throughout the entire world, and its antecedents as far as they can be traced into the backward and abysm of time, can be seen as amounting substantially to bread and wine on a table. We are hungry, and we are a family, a kind of household, whose problem is how in real communion to share what bread we have. And our evil is that we forget this. Forgetting is our undoing.

What makes life profane is forgetting, is narrow-mindedness, is restricting one's consciousness to the ego's immediate pleasure or pain. Remembering knits us up again, restores to us the sense of life's magnificence, makes us wonder if we have been wise in assuming that death has such a commanding role in our affairs. The Church has provided a ceremonial for remembering, for rescuing us from the narrow mind and the foreshortened view. In the Eucharist we give thanks for Christ, and we find that all our finer perceptions, which nothing in the material world can explain or abolish, gather round him and are held together there. This density of presence is in part what the word 'sacrament' means. As Helen Waddell said, 'even as the cup is held to your lips, divine hands are holding a diviner draught to your heart'.[3]

No one expects every Eucharist to glow with such meaning. Religious awareness fluctuates tantalizingly, sometimes fails altogether. The Church has packed enough meaning into the word 'remembrance' to fill a library, but sometimes our remembering at the Mass cannot be anything more than the effort to recall, in this present half-light in which little is clear, meanings that we just know we did once see.

In a love that lasts, two lovers through the years often lose the vivid realization of each other, the shiver of thankfulness for the other's existence, that is romance. The acceptance of such fadings of conscious delight is in itself one of the means by which love deepens and matures.

Faith grows in the same way. It would be a trivial and shallow thing if it was kept going on excitements, even excitements about God. Christians learn a strong and continuing faith the only way such a thing is ever learned, by accepting life's moodiness and its boredoms, by being happy and unhappy, and trusting the growing kingdom within.

For some years there have been important researches into religious experience, its character and incidence among people of different ages and environment and education. It appears that the definition with which these surveys operate refers to numinous and mystical experi-

[3] Quoted by Dame Felicitas of Stanbrook Abbey in a tribute to Helen Waddell (*The Tablet*, 8 January 1977)

ence, and that this is understood as primarily an awareness of the holy and an intuitive perception that all things
are one.

Such awareness and intuition are characteristic ingredients of religious experience but they certainly do not
define it. In the Christian view religious experience is not
a particular kind of event, to be distinguished from other
events in someone's life. It is one's whole life understood
in a certain way, lived 'in spirit and in truth'. That is to
say, it is the whole of one's life lived in the understanding
that the truth about what matters is to be found in Jesus,
as this truth is explored and interpreted in the Church
under the guidance of the Spirit.

So someone's 'spiritual' life is not just his moments of
clarity and conviction, his days of modest success in living
up to his Christian profession. It is the entire thing, and
includes his difficulties, failures, perplexities, his anger
(whether justified or infantile) with God, people or things
that provoke him in one way or another. William Temple
said 'Religious experience is the ordinary experience of
religious men'.[4]

Our personalities differ, and we have to accept this, and
realize that a lot of good religion will be a completely
closed book to us. Our bodies come into it. You have a
different kind of religious experience when you are on
your summer holiday from the miserable thing it is when
you have 'flu. Our minds too; when they are registering
the mystery of life's monstrous wrongness, faith does not
take the pain away; in some ways it makes it worse. There
is a core of perplexity and tension in the faith, or the
scepticism, of everyone who accepts the dignity of the
mind. It is part of ordinary life and will have its place in
the religious way of living ordinary life. Those who have

[4] William Temple, *Christus Veritas*, Macmillan 1949, p. 37

come to rely for peace of mind on a desperate incuriosity that dare not face life's more pointed questions naturally cannot see this; but they may well find themselves expecting the wrong things of religion.

Because contemporary life is so thin and lonely for so many people their secret dream tends to be of a life too bright to be human. This dream fuses with the promise of evangelists who have often offered more than Christ can give. The result is that faith has a load of expectation heaped on it that it cannot sustain. Far less harm is done by a realistic presentation, though the buyers may be fewer.

Part of Christian realism today is a necessary sensitiveness to people's difficulty in grasping much of Christianity's central beliefs. It needs to be pointed out that such difficulty may lower the tone of Christian confidence a little, but it injects a genuine vitality into the spiritual life.

Hugh Sykes Davies[5] recalls a remark of T. S. Eliot after they had been having some animated discussion with a Marxist. Eliot said that it seemed to him that there was a great difference between the Marxists and himself, as a Christian, not only in the content of their beliefs but even more in the way in which he and they both held their beliefs. He said, 'They seem so certain of what they believe. My own beliefs are held with a scepticism which I never even hope to be quite rid of.'

It is characteristic of Christian faith that it is this kind of dynamic tension in the mind rather than a static certainty. Many people do in fact want the certainty; and they are really wanting something less than faith, something easier than faith. They are wanting a kind of rest. You can have the certainty. They sell it at the various fundamentalist

[5] *T. S. Eliot, The Man and His Work*, ed. Allen Tate, Penguin 1971, p. 358

shops, from totalitarian Marxism to some brands of Christianity. Most people, however, think it an unnatural thing and not one of the covenanted mercies of God. And there's not much life in it. A character in a play by Graham Greene, speaking of faith, says, 'We are none of us *sure*. When you aren't sure, you are alive.'

II

Recollection in Tranquillity

THE first time I attended a retreat I did so simply because I was so humiliated by the thinness and vagueness of my life as a Christian believer. I had been thinking of the Saviour's words about one's light shining before men. I had difficulties with them. I was aware that I did not like people who seemed to be doing this—letting their light shine. It illuminated nothing. It increased the century's already considerable gloom. Again and again I found myself wishing he had never said those words. Certainly if I took them seriously I realized that my light was one of so few watts it was a question whether it was on or off.

In any case I rather wished to be unconcerned about myself, whether as shining light or smoking flax. All the authorities say that preoccupation with oneself is the staple diet of hell.

So I desperately wanted a fresh sense of something I thought I had had a few times in the past but not recently. It was what religious men have meant by the phrase 'the glory of God'. It seemed to me likely that I might find it again in a holy place where men and women were praying in the traditional patience and regularity and quiet of the monastic day. There must be many valid reasons for going to a retreat, but that is still the main reason why I go every year, and have done for a long time now, that I may have my sense of the glory of God renewed, and also to spend some time among those who love him, whose love has involved them in living life in such an unusual way. Their presence helps remarkably.

A subsidiary reason, though an important one, that proved itself not long after, is the need for shelter from the incessant rain of stimuli that makes such a mess of you if you stay in it too long. I am a little perplexed in exposing this need. It has to be admitted that the priest or minister is exceptionally fortunate as compared with other Christians in that he has that good thing, a room of his own, in the form of the vicarage or manse study. It is possible for him to be alone there, even if for less time than he would like or than he needs, in a place of books and quiet and various other aids to prayer. Most people live without books, most people can never be alone, most people can never be silent, unless they go some distance to find solitude and silence.[1] I who had these precious facilities, for which thousands of people envied me perhaps, found they were not enough.

Actually there was no inadequacy in these assets themselves. The trouble was that I was prevented from using them. And what stood in the way was a wild mistake I was making about the way life goes. I had always held the view that what matters in life is interest in one's existence and enthusiasm about one's work. I believed that if these obtained you could subject your mind and body to almost indefinite output, the flow of energy turned off naturally and automatically for a few hours in the twenty-four by the arrival of God's gift of sleep. I distinguished between tiredness, which has a pleasant smile on its face, and fatigue, which has a ravaged countenance; and fatigue is never produced by work, only by some secret battle going on in the mind. That was the sort of perfectionism

[1] The Association for Promoting Retreats, Church House, Newton Road, London W2, publishes details of retreats in its pamphlet *Vision* annually

with a touch of half-baked psychology I was using for fuel in those days.

I learned otherwise. No normal person has ever been free from inner conflict, not even Jesus. Why should we try to knock up a better score than his? More importantly, life needs rhythm and alternation if it is to come consistently good and not drain from you the precious sense of freedom to be yourself. If you don't balance your immersion in the interests and claims of life with withdrawals from them, you reduce the amount of yourself that is available to you. You live with less and less of yourself. Indeed you live with what is an increasingly automatic self and a feeble echo of your everyday world, so that it becomes a question whether you, as God wills you, exist at all, or just something the twentieth century has made of you.

Every period has its own general atmosphere of suggestion and implication and disguised expressions of value and fear. This constitutes the air which everyone breathes. The twentieth century's mental climate is largely the creation of television and radio, advertising and the press, a process continually gaining in latitude and power.

These mass media present us with abstractions all the time, abstractions in the sense of segments of reality cut out of the whole and presented to the mind with such daily persistence and such skill that we are conditioned into thinking that that is our mediocre, or frightful, world. The Christian does not deny that the world contains the trivial, the bizarre, the criminal, the perverse, of whose presence the media continually remind us. What he complains about, and he is not the only one who complains, is what is omitted. What is omitted is precisely the sort of thing St Paul argued should be constantly in the

foreground of the mind—the good, the true, the beautiful, the amusing, the happy, the congenially and typically human, and humanity's inability to stop longing for
life to mean something and to light up with love.

The only way to realize the existence of this other half
of reality is to pull out of the world dominated by the
mass media and go somewhere where you will be
reminded of the things that shape the dignity and hope of
life, and have some freedom and peace to reflect on
them.

The Church in its regular worship is supposed to be
providing such reminder, such opportunity for reflec-
tion. It is rather a large size in admissions to acknowledge
that on the whole the Church today does not offer this
kind of fare. Apart from the great centres of worship,
public prayer today does not revive the sense of life's
meaning and its inherent goodness. The general run of
church services and the weekly programme of church
activities do not enlighten and sustain as they may have
done in the past. It could be that this programme is in fact
being swept into the general flux of the waters of change
in which we are all struggling to keep afloat, and that God
has some better thing in store for us.

There may be indications of coming new patterns in the
fact that many people find the short intensive period of
worship, prayer, instruction or study more of a means of
grace than the protracted and diluted programme characteristic of church life in the past. There is a remarkable and
growing interest in the world of contemplation. There has
also appeared in recent years the need for a more personal
faith, and for more personal help with this longing for
God that is such a peculiar mixture of irritation and joy,
something along the lines of what used to be called
'spiritual direction' together with the kind of

enlightening dialogue that is a feature of the analytical situation.

Once you have jettisoned second-hand views about religion and begun your own search, you discover that we are more completely and sensitively ourselves, in our individuality, before God than in anyone else's presence, even that presence we love more intensely than any other in the human world. Much of the time a false self is operating and making the real self conform to its requirements. When you start your own search for God, the real you begins to look up and take charge. It may well be the first time it has ever had a chance.

That self has its own freedom and authority. It knows instinctively that much of what it has been given in the world of religion is about as much use as Saul's armour. It sets out with a very little; but its mood is alert, and it wants to learn. It feels 'this is me'. There is a fastidiousness that is quite compatible with humility. It is the other side of the coin of selfhood. And it wants its own private needs and horrors to be understood.

So it is not surprising that people are finding that they need less group activity and more opportunity of conversation with a single individual, who has time at his disposal, is also interested in the search inwards, and does not breathe only ecclesiastical and theological air.

It is easy to see that the retreat, while in no sense a new form of spiritual life, meets much of this current religious need so satisfactorily that it is not surprising that most organized retreats are soon fully booked. My own preference is for the traditional form, and I grumble at every attempt to reduce the silence, but I am sure that counsellings are likely to be an increasingly important element in retreats of the future. This means that the conductor needs to have not only general understanding of the

Christian way of praying but also a very flexible imagination so that he can truly sympathize with the different
ways in which the desire for God seizes people today. He
needs the grace of a quick insight into a particular individual's condition and some skill as an instructor in
prayer who can make use of the new ways in which people
want to pray nowadays. We understand that the full-time
priests of tomorrow are going to be far fewer than in the
past. If they are trained to be specialists of this kind they
will be very much in demand; but they will certainly need
to be trained, because an entirely new language needs to
be learned for speaking about the spiritual life, a brighter,
fresher, more interesting form of religious conversation
than seems to be at present at the Church's command.

One of the advantages of making one's retreat in a
religious community is that the daily Offices in the chapel
have each its individual meaning and all together become
symbol; they bring you face to face with time, the swift-
ness of time, the shortness of time, the brightening, fad-
ing, wasting of life, from earliest light until at Compline
we all meet to call it a day.

Time cannot be seen as meaning anything by people
who allow themselves to be completely immersed in it.
The more one is swept along in the high wind of time the
more life loses meaning, because one cannot get one's
thoughts into any kind of order in that phenomenal
storm. If meaning is to be seen in time, if it is to be
recovered when lost, there must be detachment, there
must be recollection, somewhere to stand and be still.

Tennessee Williams has observed that when we sense
the significance and depth of a great play it is because we
are contemplating *the arrest of time* in a completed work
of art. A critic had remarked of Miller's play *Death of a
Salesman* that its principal character, Willy Loman, was

'the sort of man that almost any member of the audience would have kicked out of an office had he applied for a job or detained one for conversation about his troubles'.

The author replied how true this judgement is in the world of offices, appointments, diaries and job-hunting, but that if we could encounter Willy Loman somehow outside that secular context, outside time, the temporal pressures off for a while, we would receive him with 'concern and kindness and even with respect'.

This is what happens to us in the world of the theatre. The world of a play offers us the view of certain people under the special conditions of a world without time. It has a certain repose 'which allows contemplation and produces the climate in which tragic importance is a possible thing'.[2]

Art and prayer have this in common, that they are means of restoring dignity to life through detachment and repose, by giving us the chance to see importance and meaning again. In the Eucharist we are able to say the *Sanctus* precisely because we have lifted up our hearts, because we have mentally pulled out of mere time; we have entered the dimension of faith in which everything is lovable again because it is seen to be happening within the kingdom of God.

The opposite of detachment is obsession. Obsession is the centre of many of our miseries. Anxiety, resentment, regret, three of our most familiar devils, are forms of obsession. The thought of one particular evil comes to the foreground of the mind, pushes away the other pleasanter things we might think, becomes all we are thinking about, and we are at its mercy. Wisdom would seem to be not a facility for excluding anxiety, resentment and regret, because that would mean denying facts, disowning a part

[2] Tennessee Williams, *The Rose Tattoo*, Penguin Books 1968, pp. 11–14

of oneself. Wisdom is a matter of letting the black thought come (one probably has no choice about this) yet keeping a margin all round it in the mind, so that it is seen in relation to other thoughts, other facts of life, which make it look less formidable.

With experience this ability grows. As one grows older one begins to register the number of times when fears, obsessive and swamping anxieties, never turned out to be as ghastly as one imagined beforehand. One learns a kind of mental flexibility in virtue of which one can bring the fear, the hate, whatever it is, into compensating and enlightening relation to better-looking features of one's life.

Still, many of us know this to be a losing battle. The mind's tendency to stall in obsession, in vague anxiety or particular grief, increases its hold, What a blessing it is then, what a need, to get away, to be for a few days in a new and unfamiliar routine, among people about whom one knows absolutely nothing except that they too want to recover emotional spontaneity, and to see one's life in the wide setting of the Christian considerations set before us by the conductor, the worship of the community, the reading, the quiet.

There is progress too in the understanding of prayer itself. Too often we tend to think of prayer as speech, or some form of voicing our requests to God. So intercession becomes a message to God to help the person who is just now in our conscious love, as though we do the asking and God does the helping. I have come to think of prayer for others as a peculiarly paradoxical thing. It is often a form of intensest love, indeed it is the only air in which some forms of love can freely breathe. Yet it is also a form of detachment, and it must be this to be Christian.

To pray for someone in the Christian way is to detach ourselves from our anxieties and preferences concerning this person and to love him in the largest possible world of love. That is to say, it is to love him within our thankfulness that God's love is the most real and indestructible thing in the world, and then to offer ourselves to God for the carrying out of any part of his purpose for this beloved individual that he may lay upon us. Praying is intensely personal and at the same time a shedding of the merely and narrowly personal, so that it becomes a kind of 'recollection in tranquillity'. In this way it purifies and educates love. It is hard to pray in the Christian way for someone for whom one's love contains an overweight of self-regarding dependency.

Retreats are experiences that require a certain courage in making the best use of them. On their first retreat people sometimes discover with a shock how frightening silence can be, its unexpected power to show us our emptiness. Virginia Woolf in her *A Writer's Diary*[3] wrote:

> Often down here I have entered into a sanctuary; a nunnery: had a religious retreat; of great agony once; and always some terror; so afraid one is of loneliness; of seeing to the bottom of the vessel. That is one of the experiences I have had here in some Augusts—and got then to a consciousness of what I call 'reality': a thing I see before me: something abstract but residing in the downs or sky, beside which nothing matters, in which I shall rest and continue to exist. Reality I call it. And I fancy sometimes this is the most necessary thing to me, that which I seek.

In retreat one certainly can have this experience of seeing 'to the bottom of the vessel' and wondering whether what you are is no more than something the slightest wind could blow away and out of existence as commonly understood. I believe, however, that such critical and searching and in the end creative experience

[3] Hogarth Press 1969, p. 132

does not come before you are ready for it and can make use of it.

God does not lead us into any experience that is not, in his providential care, right for us at that particular time, if only we are willing to learn his truth. One needs to be willing to learn. I do not see how we can learn anything at all from any kind of experience unless we do indeed wish to learn from it. Anyone who is willing to give up the time to go to a retreat is usually someone who wants to learn, and to learn from the deepest possible source, that reality in whose arrangement all our lives mysteriously stand, who is said to be seeking us all the time, though he has no distance at all to go, wanting us to want him as much as he wants us.

Certainly for those whose working day is normally accompanied by continuous radio, a silent retreat is a very considerable change of air, like attempting to live solo, without support. They are sure to be restless for a while, as some urban types, visiting the deep countryside, find the night a soft dark void that oppresses them and keeps them awake. But gradually the spirit of the place takes hold, the mind settles, there is an acceptance of the unfamiliar conditions, which begin to seem like peace itself as, after each Office or address, the silence washes back like a returning tide. Soon time becomes less urgent, less domineering. Each day dawdles through, but it does not bore. You get on better terms with yourself and find that what you are thinking and feeling is more interesting than you expected. There is the pleasant surprise of the quite palpable intimacy with the other retreatants without the exchange of a single word.

It would be difficult to overestimate the importance of this journey into silence in the journey of faith. There is no hope of getting anywhere unless you work your way

behind the appearances and superficialities of the world of
religion. The appearances are the clichés, the platitudes,
the picture-book imagery, denominational prejudices,
unexamined moral preconceptions, banal sentiments, and
rituals whose vitality is as impressive as that which throbs
in the faces in Madame Tussaud's.

Outside the Church this superficial world consists of
all the conventional anti-religion of the twentieth century. It is a mock-up of pretentious humanism, self-
righteous atheism, facile moralism, which altogether
never seems to produce that stimulating criticism of religion which such forces ought to be marshalling in the
interests of truth, for our sakes as well as theirs.   And
there is the unexamined adulation of science which keeps
our generation from the light of truth. The word 'science'
simply means 'knowledge'. As such it is a fine word,
doing a very important job in the conversation of humanity. But there is a view of it which restricts it unjustifiably,
and tends to give 'pre-eminence to those sciences that
appear important only from the point of view of a vul-
garized society that has become alienated from nature,
domesticated, cut off from traditional values and given to
measuring solely in terms of commercial values. . . . "Big
Science" in no way implies a science concerned with the
most important things on our planet, nor is it the science
of the human psyche and intellect: it is exclusively that
science which promises money, energy or power, even
if it is only the power destroying the really great and
beautiful.'[4]

Anyone wanting God, hungry for an authentic religious experience, has to extricate himself from all this
that blinds and chokes his seeking spirit. And one of the
ways through is silence.

[4] Konrad Lorenz, *Civilised Man's Eight Deadly Sins*, Methuen 1974, p. 69

The rightness of silent response to the mystery of God is one of the oldest religious certainties. No one tried harder than St Augustine to say what he thought the word 'God' means, no one has brought a richer imagination to the struggle, or failed so gloriously, but fail he did again and again, with concluding sighs like 'And with all this, what have I said, my God and my Life and my sacred Delight? What can anyone say when he speaks of Thee?'[5] 'For God is more truly thought than he is uttered, and exists more truly than he is thought.'[6]

Of all the churches it is Orthodoxy that is most sensitive to this fascinating depth of religious experience, this surmise that there is an 'anti-theology' that must be allowed its critical role in any theology that is Christian. It is good both for conventional conservative evangelicalism and conventional radicalism to suspect that 'one's creed is in a sense one's tragedy, that whenever we begin talking about God we are necessarily falsifying him, that truth and life become too good to be true when they have been translated into words and that, at the same time, man is most unhappy when all is told. Silence should at last take the place of the continuous prattle and rambling about God . . . indeed silence is of the very nature of theology . . . it is something positive, like love, death and life. It is not a pause between noises, sermons and theological disquisitions, but something without which words lose their meaning.'[7]

It was St Augustine again, and his mother, together in a moment of truth that miraculously left behind all the inadequacies that haunt the love between mother and son, who realized that the fullest joy possible to us all, an

[5] St Augustine, *Confessions*, 1:4
[6] *On the Trinity*, V11:4.7
[7] Eugene Lampert, *The Orthodox Ethos*, vol. 1, p. 222

entering into the joy that is at the heart of the universe, would be a passing beyond words and images and every transient sign to that silence in which we could hear the love we are all seeking, 'not by any tongue of flesh nor the voice of an angel nor the sound of thunder nor in the darkness of a parable'[8] but Himself, in a moment of understanding for which the whole world sighs. Unique as this is, we are in the approaches to it at any rate whenever our lives are shaken by intense love or the evanescent beauty of the world and we are swept far beyond the drag and need of words.

There are many silences, 'calm and distressed'. There is the wordlessness to which people are driven by some kinds of suffering. It spills over into the life of sympathy. The people who are most use to us in the most terrible moments are likely to be those who have themselves been lonely and helpless in the crumbling of hope, or in the hurt of some want God allows but cannot satisfy, and know that where there is much to be endured there may well be little to be said.

Some praying is like this, faith's entry into the silence of God to the questions of man. That silence is entirely misunderstood if it is thought to signify God's absence; it is a form of the presence, and to be encountered and explored. Life is in places so complicated that some of the questions we ask about it are never going to be answered. There are torments and miseries that are not going to look any better however far and fiercely we pursue our search for whoever is to blame. To the angry question about who was guilty in one particularly outrageous area of human wretchedness Jesus replied that there was no answer to that kind of request for that kind of information. There would however be a kind of answer in our doing what the

[8] St Augustine, *Confessions*, tr. F. J. Sheed, Sheed and Ward 1960, p. 158

47

situation required for it to begin to come right; and when we do that we are, with Christ, the light of the world.[9]

There are more simple experiences, of injury between lovers or friends, for example, when nevertheless emotion has been so long at its distorting work that neither side is ever going to be able to recall the original situation accurately enough for the other to accept it as a fair description of the moment of hurt or humiliation or whatever. How did it all start? They cannot now know the answer. But in that silence they may come to see that, memory being so untrustworthy, forgiveness should be given at least its chance to save the situation and stop the waste of all their future.

Ladislaus Boros says that Jesus' whole existence was ruled by a great silence, because he was all the time unreservedly receptive, alert to the presence of opportunities that give life another chance. I wish I had been taught as much about this silent Jesus as I have about Jesus the teacher.

I believe that human imagination is marvellously fed by silence. Some of the acceptances that give life dignity seem to come from it, some lessening of our fears. It is also a sign. It points to the meaning that spiritual men have always seen in stillness and emptiness. Lives that are deprived of it lose out on other important things. The way the Church will make this clear is not by saying it but by providing it, in religious communities, in retreat houses, and in spaces of silence in its regular worship long enough for people to wonder what is happening. They might usefully be told that Kierkegaard once said, with characteristic exaggeration and relevance, 'Silences are the only scrap of Christianity we still have left'.

[9] St John, 9:1–5

III

The Following Plough

As the plough follows words,
so God rewards prayers.
                —WILLIAM BLAKE

HOW we set about praying for people depends on what we think any kind of praying is for.

If you want to change the world, even if it is just to improve circumstances in one small area of life's sadness and injustice, prayer is not the first thing to which you would naturally turn. It seems to me that the sensible thing to do would be to find out what forces in society are already set to bring about the changes you desire and then to discover how you could ally yourself with those good people in co-operative action.

If, however, you are trying to see such circumstances as in some sense to do with God and bearing God in them, if you want to recall your deepest understanding of life and strengthen your religious self's hold on it so that you can find the presence of God in your circumstances whatever they are, then you would naturally think of praying.

I am sure that many Christians find difficulty in this way of putting the matter. They feel it rather skirts round the point of the exercise. They want to be assured that when we pray for others it does some good to the person prayed for. I do not know that this assurance can be given them, or indeed from what source it could come. I believe that good is done, that God uses all the love and faith of the prayer and weaves them into the garment of time. That particular belief, however, is a matter of faith. The precise way in which God uses ('answers') the prayer is not open to verification, because such verifications are not part of the life of faith. The idea that it is possible to

show the relation, or just that there is in fact some relation, between a given quantity and kind of prayer and an
event in the natural world, seems to me to be mistaken.

The mental atmosphere a Christian breathes is not of
that kind. It does not contain such assurances because it
does not contain that sort of god—a god who is an observable object or force among other observable objects and
forces, only the top one, the one endowed with most
power. That sort of god is what William Blake called 'the
external god, an allegory of kings and nothing else'.

Because it is impossible to prove that any prayer has
ever been 'answered', it is also the case that one never
prays because one is persuaded by the results of prayer
(one's own or other people's) that it is worth while. What
happens as a result of my praying for others does not give
me faith in prayer. My praying is the result of my faith, of
how I understand what happens, what is happening all the
time. And what is happening all the time is that God is
continually present in life's good and evil, that is to say,
the God and Father of our Lord Jesus Christ. His presence colours everything. Faith is a journey in and into the
realization of that; and prayer is one of the things a
religious person does to sharpen that realization so that he
can bear it more and more, come to be glad in it, extend
his response to that mysterious and tremendous presence.

Consequently, one of my early perplexities was the
discovery of the extent to which, in the life of the Church,
intercessory prayer has come to be rather obsessed with
physical illness. Though I am glad that there are special
groups in the Church devoted to intercession for the sick,
I have difficulties about those entirely existing for this
purpose. One is that I have seen that such groups have too
limited a programme for intrinsic interest to be main-
tained. They tend to wilt, to sink into uninspired obli-

gation, and then to die rather guiltily. More importantly, they seem to be making too much of a subsidiary aspect of the spiritual life, upsetting the balance of things in the advertisement of Christianity.

As I understand Christianity, it is a religion principally (but very deeply) concerned with people's inner life, with their hopes, wants, angers, dreads, and above all with the possibility of their ever loving as they long to love, with getting people's loving released from all that imprisons and suffocates it and out into the open world where human beings simply wait for it to come their way.

On this understanding of the life of faith, it is clear that physical illness, even fatal illness, should be regarded as not necessarily as great an evil as, say, becoming convinced that life is meaningless, or living day after day hating someone, or being dogged by some fear that you can never track down. Certainly there are difficulties in the way of bringing such terrors into the public prayer of the Church. But the way we pray in Church should not give the impression that we believe that someone who is ill with bronchitis is a more suitable subject for the prayers of the Church than those others whose miseries may be merely spiritual (and incidentally the main concern of the Church) but are just as painful as the body's pain but much lonelier because necessarily hidden.

I suspect that this preoccupation with physical illness suggests an idea of prayer as a means of enlisting the help of God in the alteration of external situations, as though, in the case of illness for example, he is some superior doctor more skilled than anyone in the BMA. That would mean both that we are attempting to use God and also that we are misreading the way he expresses his providential care.

The healing ministry of Jesus in the New Testament is

misunderstood when people think it has been given in its entirety to the Church of today. It is ludicrous to say that because certain kinds of healing appear in the New Testament the Church today must also heal in those ways.

Jesus lived and worked in a pre-scientific world. Since his day the healing power of God has been shed abroad in the world in a marvellous diversity of ways. One of the most marvellous is the development of scientific medicine.

As a result of this, for example, we expect a disease of the eyes to be healed by recourse to ophthalmic surgery, not by the use of prayer, much less by the application of clay and spittle (St John 9:6–7).

The healing of the sick body of humanity now proceeds by both external and inward means as a great complex miracle in which scientific medicine, the social sciences, religion, education and all the many varieties of human idealism and compassion play their different parts.

Christian faith believes that it is the Lord's doing; it is marvellous in our eyes, and it continually forms the substance of the praying Church's thanksgiving and desire.

When Christians make some part of life's sickness or wrongness a matter of prayer it is not because they think that when they pray they plug in to some supernatural power that does things in selected places. That is an exceedingly unfortunate road for faith. We shall be inclined to praise God when things in our view go right and to be dismayed at him and doubtful of his credibility when things in our view go wrong.

The result of our restricting our view of things in this infantile way is our forgetting that in any given situation the complex structure of God's mercy may require a very different form of his presence from the one for which our hearts at the moment happen to ache. The wiser course is to choose a more relaxed and flexible approach.

Christians pray for others because they find that their way of loving so behaves. We bring the person we love, or the cause that is our concern, into all that Christ has taught us about God and his desire for a world in which human beings care for one another. We make the connection between such caring and our understanding of God's ways and our wish to do something that he can take into his extraordinary love for the stammering and stumbling that is our human acknowledgement of his reality. We bring our loving into the warmth and width of our personal world of faith.

And then things happen. The situation or problem or need looks different in the light of God's purpose. Many other considerations are allowed to have a bearing on it, as when someone, out in the country, stops using his field-glasses and lets the object he is looking at so closely appear again as part of a landscape.

In this wider view we often realize that some at any rate of the answer to our prayer could rightly come through us. We hear the God of situations calling to us for the service that will carry that part of his answer.

There are situations, however, in which the intractability of life or the insufficiency of human knowledge and skill dominate the scene like a doom. Our prayer then becomes one with the pain of all who have ever waited in dismay, knocking helplessly at some door that never opened.

We are told that God is more ready to hear than we are to pray. We can accept that. That does seem like us. Because, however, he works his will through persons, many of his answers wait on the availability of people willing to carry them from the world of heaven to the world of earth.

There are always some people prepared to give him what he wants, a certain number who are willing to be bearers of his tremendous purpose, but it is a smallish group compared with the other sort. Jesus seems to have had despairing thoughts about this when he observed how few labourers seem to be around for the plenteous harvest of God's unfathomable love.

If people say that they want more from religion than this, more guarantees that it works, I think they are a long way from the truth as it is in Jesus. They need to have another look at the cross.

His was not an easy religion. If it was we would despise him and it and turn him out of our lives as a man whose fancy words (as those of too many preachers) do not fit the facts.

Much 'working', upholding, reassuring there is in his religion, but it comes from wanting to be part of his world of love and faith whether we live or die. It comes from entering more deeply into what it means to be his.

He did not always get what he wanted. Facing that, trying to accept and make some sense and use of not getting what you want, trying to understand why indeed so many people in the world are shut out of what they so reasonably desire, is an essential part of Christian praying.

One of our great perplexities just now is the terribly intractable situation in Northern Ireland and the many Christian prayers that have been offered for its ending.

Whatever else such prayers effect, they are a natural means of seeing that situation in the light of faith. Our faith is that God's purpose is to bring that horrible situation to an end, but only through a great complex of political decisions and economic arrangements and relig-ious accommodations which men with God's help must make. That is certainly the way God usually seems to work.

If men will not make such decisions and arrangements under the guidance of the Spirit, God will not solve the problem on his own.

There is a saying of Jesus' that is more than usually haunting. 'Blessed is he who is not offended in me.' It is a saying that fits well into our thought of God himself in whose wisdom things in this world are as they so strangely are. Blessed is he who is not offended at the way God goes on, at what he allows, at the time he takes to get anything done.

To pray for others is part of the Christian way of loving. If it is a true loving, and not a disguised statement of our possessiveness or fear, it will also be a form of detachment.

Suppose we realize that someone we love is threatened, is in some physical or spiritual danger, or lacks something he needs and we want him to have, and we pray for him. If our prayer rises out of our unexamined anxieties and preferences it may well be an expression of fear and projection rather than love. If so, it will be immature praying because it is poor loving. To love is to be able and ready to do that part of God's purpose for this loved individual that he may lay upon us. We shall not in fact be able and ready to do that if our fears are preoccupying and depressing us.

To love someone must also mean seeing him as he is, in his true self, and to want him to grow and mature in his own way, according to his needs, not ours. It means being able to read the message hidden in the code of his behaviour and to understand (it may be) the lonely grievance or fear or the longing for freedom that is obscurely signalling.

And love that is Christian love continually renews its thankfulness that God is nearer than anyone to the people we love, using their lives to make known to them the meaning of those lives and his place in that meaning. The situation that has stirred us to pray for this person has as its major significance the fact that it may hinder or assist his growth in love, his fulfilment in God.

Prayer for someone that is a form of Christian loving will be prayer that sets him within our readiness to act, our objective concern, our imaginative sympathy and our faith in God's surrounding care.

This is why there is some help in seeing intercession as a form of contemplation. It is, in part at any rate, a kind of becoming aware of the real situation, as faith sees it when the distorting mist that fearing and wanting pour over it has been dispelled.

This new seeing may well be a very practical and efficient form of loving. Someone in the Society of Friends' tradition of spirituality has written:

> The situation or person may well be in need of our help, but we may not know the best way to give it. Perhaps our initial response should be 'How can I understand?' rather than 'What can I do?' . . . Seen thus, the criminal does not cry out to be reformed, the alcoholic to be cured, the atheist to be converted. It is our loving, uncritical acceptance which may be called for in the first instance, undistorted by our desire to put him right, to have him conform to *our* notion of desirable behaviour, or to do him good. We may then be better placed to discover what the most effective action might be, and how best we can serve him.[1]

There are of course many situations in which there

[1] Ralph Hetherington, *The Sense of Glory*, Friends Home Service 1975, p. 66

seems to be nothing that we can directly do. Even so, it is still true that every turning to God in prayer is met with his response. He uses it in the fulfilment of his purpose *at some point* in its manifold range. This idea becomes clearer when it is brought alongside the thought of God's presence.

In all that happens God is present, though not all that happens carries his presence in its fulness. In the event that we consider evil, all that we may be able to see of his presence is his permission that life in this place should just now have this dreadful character. He is also present in the redeemability that lies deep within every evil. It is part of the goodness of life that every evil carries this whisper of God. He is indeed everywhere. There is a psalm that says that even if you made your bed in hell you would lie down with God.

So God is present in every situation, but he is more amply and effectively present whenever anyone there turns to him in faith and love. Human trust in God and willingness to be used by him give his presence in the world a power it would not otherwise have, since God has chosen to heal life's wounds and reconcile its contradictions through the affection and courage and patience of men and women.

When someone we love is suffering some form of life's wrongness or is in some special need or maybe is in no need at all and it is just that we love him and want God to use our love for his good, we pray for him. In answer to our prayer God may give us something to do for this person. If there is nothing we can directly do for him there is bound to be something similar that we can do for someone else, or something that we know would please and encourage him were he to see love brightening the world in that way. All loving increases the fulness of

God's presence in the world and so brings him nearer to anyone and everyone.

It is difficult to explain how a small act of love (a prayer, for example) in one place can make possible or add to greater good far away. All we can say is that we believe that God's work of healing and reconciliation is one because he is one. The power of an act of love is not confined to the occasion that focuses it. It becomes one with God's universal presence of love. Eventually God's purpose to bring to an end the trouble in Northern Ireland will be fulfilled. Among the constituents of that process, in its infinite diversity, will be the attempts of countless ordinary people outside Ireland to conquer their own religious and political prejudices. Every intolerance thought through and dissolved, every irrational fear examined and dismissed, has its place in the world's enlightenment, is ground gained for all the rest.

The intercessions in the Eucharist are a form of contemplating this oneness of life within God's love, that we are all in it together and whatever we do helps or hinders the others. To pray for another person means to hold together our love for the person we want to help and our faith in God's presence in his life. We complete the prayer by offering ourselves to God to be the channel of any part of his blessing he sees we can carry, either directly to this person or in suitable loving action of other kinds. There is always something we can do to increase the manifest power of that divine reality in which both we and the one we love are held.

Faith and love are the important things, and the readiness to hold to God through good and ill. What stands in the way is fear, and the demand that God shall meet our particular requests. It is good to ask God to take out of our prayer all such dread, all such insistence that his blessing conform to our ideas of what the situation requires. They will indeed automatically diminish the stronger our faith becomes. When faith is strong it is able to come to rather surprising conclusions, like this, for example:

> I know that good is coming to me—that good is always coming; though few have at all times the simplicity and courage to believe it. What we call evil is the only and best shape which, for the person and his condition at the time, could be assumed by the best good.[2]

I am certainly not able to say that I think it is easy to believe that. I can, however, say that I believe that, if God is what Jesus said he is, something like it must be true. I often read it and think about it. As I give myself time and quietness to think about it I find my mind more and more ready to receive it.

---

[2] George Macdonald, *Phantastes*, Chatto and Windus 1913, p. 217

IV

On Dryness

THERE is a strange poem of T. S. Eliot called *The Hollow Men*. He wrote it after *The Waste Land*, and it is rather like a coda to the grave music of that poem, a coda of bizarre dryness and beauty. It ends with peculiar haltings and hesitations in the world of unsuccessful prayer, where the attempt to pray and the failure to pray seem to take melancholy turns. The desire to pray, to say the Lord's Prayer, is shown as struggling through the persistent experience of inhibition, through our sense that something (Eliot calls it the Shadow) continually comes between our aspirations and their fulfilment. The poem ends in a kind of spiritual stumbling

> For thine is
> Life is
> For thine is the

and it falters away in a childish jingle about the world ending not with a bang but a whimper.

It has always seemed to me a truly religious poem, of the universal kind that unites people of any religion and none. Everyone knows the presence of the Shadow, the way our longing to reach out to others is challenged by our bondage to ourselves, our thirst for the ideal by our preoccupation with the trivial. The religious person finds that faith introduces him to a particularly sharp and continuing encounter with this contradiction in things.

Reference to this struggle with the Shadow haunts

Christian writing on the journey of faith. So Cardinal Newman, setting down his reflexions during a retreat, went on at length about his spiritual inadequacies, how much official religion oppressed him, how little enthusiasm he could summon for the things of God, 'like a man who is trying to walk with his legs tied together . . . as though I were bound with chains'. The Shadow pursued him through the years. 'As the years go on, I have less and less sensible devotion and inward life.' And he wondered gloomily whether old men's souls must be 'as stiff, as lean, as bloodless as their bodies, except so far as grace penetrates and softens them. And it requires a flooding of grace to do this.'[1]

This condition of being bored with the spiritual life and finding prayer just about the last thing one wants to do has always molested people who have wanted God. In the principal attempts to describe the Christian journey it has usually been considered under the term 'aridity', or dryness. It is possible to give it both too much and too little importance.

The failure of spontaneity, having to drive oneself to the job in hand, is often not important enough to require any consideration. To put it under the spiritual microscope would be like making a moral issue out of Monday morning. No doubt every inertia can be traced to the secret longing to return to the womb, but people inclined to fraternize with such ultimates soon find themselves out of touch with life. At the other extreme is the listless spirit and black thoughts which make life seem like a dark stairway you are mounting on your hands and knees. That is not dryness, or even the dark night of the soul. It is depression.

Between these two extremes of insignificant inertia and

[1] J. H. Newman, *Meditations and Devotions*, p. 597

pathological fatigue is this common religious condition of not wanting to pray and finding little enthusiasm and conviction when one attempts it. An obvious producer of it is physical illness. There are people, perhaps not many, of a rather exacting fervour, who deplore their slackening hold on spiritual realities when they are ill. It has to be a sensitive and sympathetic reassurance that gets through to them.

More sinisterly, if guilt nags at us, if we are ill at ease about unconfessed sin or confessed sin we are not seeking to amend, the odds are that this inner restlessness will make us unwilling to look God in the face in prayer.

St John of the Cross had very interesting ideas on the likelihood that the drying up of prayer is a sign that a change of style in one's spiritual life is necessary. People sometimes find themselves pervaded by a great dissatisfaction with religion, the normal fare which the Church and their own spiritual routine have offered their mind and imagination is now quite useless, yet they still want God. They know they want him because no alternative or distraction obscures their sense that God is the only inspiration, the only rebuke they care about, and his remoteness is the only distance that makes them feel they are alone, yet they find it impossible to think *about* him. When this happens, St John says, it may well mean that they should turn to contemplative prayer. That may seem a rather technical matter, but in today's widespread interest in contemplation it certainly has a fresh and more general relevance which is likely to lead to new interpretations.

The dryness that is a kind of contemplation-starvation is a quite different range of religious experience from that which St John calls 'the dark night of the soul'. He uses this famous image in association with his idea of a

Christian's spiritual growth as an affair of three phases. These phases, if I have understood him, are not to be seen as only successive. As they are lived they overlap, there are regressions, there are anticipations of the later in the earlier, since spiritual life is the life of a human being. But it is useful to distinguish them in theory.

The first is the freeing of the self from the misdirection of energy and misunderstanding of the truth about God and life that form our pre-conversion state. The second is the arrival of a recognizable confidence, knowledge of oneself and of God, and commitment to God. The third stage, for those who achieve it, is when the individual's life is integrated and simplified in the love of God and openness to him.

Between stages one and two, and between stages two and three there is a crisis of reluctance for which St John used this 'dark night' image.

The reluctance is one of discouragement, fear and temptation, discouragement at one's apparent lack of progress and at the inadequacy of what one so far has got out of faith, fear of becoming too religious—in the double sense of being afraid of what God may ask of us if we get too near him and of the eccentricities and blindnesses into which our enthusiasm, if given its head, will lead us, and temptation to settle at some manageable level, to take religion no farther than this. It needs courage and energy to sustain these pressures and plod on.

Incidentally, this three-phase pattern appears fre-quently elsewhere. Sometimes clear in the development of human personality as it matures from young adulthood to old age, it is certainly visible in the work of many artists, such as Shakespeare, Schubert, Beethoven, Rembrandt, Monet. It is marvellously shown in Beet-hoven's spiritual pilgrimage as his thought and feeling deepen through their well-defined three periods. The 'Hammerklavier' sonata was written between his second and third periods, in an extraordinary depth of anguish before he entered the reconciliation and serenity of his 'unitive' way. The tremendous *adagio sostenuto* and final fugue of that sonata are a revelation of a man wrestling with God in the dark night of the soul which is as profound as it is beautiful, as life-affirming as it is God-affirming, to whom and to Beethoven and to the inventors of the pianoforte be glory *in saecula saeculorum.*

St John also uses the idea of night as a metaphor for the normal state of faith. He chose the term not because faith is normally a gloom and an anguish, which it certainly is not, but because normally faith is not accompanied by confirming signs in the feelings. Usually as you journey in faith there are no clear evidences or obvious landmarks to assure you that you are on the right road. Faith is not a kind of knowledge or a type of sensation that is denied to people who do not believe in God. As far as the feelings are concerned, faith is more like a step by step journey in the dark.

It is a good moment in anyone's journey of faith when he discovers this classical position which so clearly distinguishes faith and feeling. Faith is what matters. If pleasant feelings come, there is every reason to be thankful, but it is unwise to give them much authority and it is a waste of time to hanker after them when they go. Dom John Chapman once gave this advice, 'You still imagine that you are not serving God properly when you are in dryness. Make up your mind once for all that dryness is best, and you will find that you are frightened at having anything else!'[2]

Learning how to distinguish and evaluate faith and

[2] The Spiritual Letters of Dom John Chapman, Sheed and Ward 1944, p. 99

feeling is a highly significant part of the first phase in the journey of faith, in which many misunderstandings about religion have to be cleared away. It is work that is never completely done, because one so often forgets and regresses into confusing the two, especially if one has a make-up that seems to need emotional rides.

As we try to understand ourselves one of our earliest surprises is what a sensitive and responsive apparatus we have in our feelings. They are affected very variously by temperament, physical health, stage of life, intellectual perplexity, testing experience. Their power is of course dramatic in the two realms in which our most important living is done. One is the world of relationship where men and women want one another but are tantalized by the swing of yearning and fear, and the other is the even more mysterious realm constituted by our elusive but never disproved sense of God. In these worlds, where the weather can be so cloudy and so brilliant, our feelings are sometimes good guides but they can be remarkable deceivers.

All of which means that there is an ebb and flow of enthusiasm in the spiritual life which has to be accepted and expected and not given too much importance. On the other hand, it does not mean that there is nothing to be done. Anyone who wants God has to take responsibility for having this want within him even though he did not put it there; he has to do things that will help.

What helps one God-seeker does not necessarily help the next. But I have found it essential to see that one has as much variety as possible in one's spiritual life. Any life is boring if its range of interest and experience is too limited. The life of faith is no exception to this rule. Much of average church life is indescribably dull, many people find it unbearable unless they can find some directing or organizing role in it, and indeed anyone who thinks that by itself receptive participation in the weekly progamme will slake his thirst for God is quite mistaken. If you want God as a reality, exciting you to gratitude, love, reverence, exasperation, incomprehension, peace (now and then), and much else that makes up the fulness of religious experience as our tradition knows that thing, there is work you have to do yourself and with yourself. And part of it is seeing to the provision of change and the stimulation of interest in the life of your religious imagination. It is quite probable that the old monastic torpor, known in the middle ages as 'acedia' (from a Greek word meaning 'indifference') was often simply boredom created by the monotony and lack of variety in medieval monastic life. Much Christian dryness today is in fact boredom and indicates the need for more varied spiritual fare than one is getting.

It is also a help to take note of the deadness in the general atmosphere of the period we live in. Not that there is any solace in such awareness, but, since the world of religion never escapes current discontents, it is sensible to be alert to the malaise of the times and to allow for its influence in our assessment of things.

We live in an age in which the traditional religious view of life has lost most of its power. Most people's thoughts refer to short-term if not immediate ends. There is what the sociologist Konrad Lorenz has called 'an impatient demand for instant gratification of all budding wishes'. The other side of the coin is the way the development of modern technology and particularly pharmacology enables us to avoid even minor unpleasurable experience.[3] There is a loss of capacity to invest hard work in undertakings whose full satisfaction is in the future and involves

[3] Konrad Lorenz, *Civilized Man's Eight Deadly Sins*, Methuen 1974, pp. 26, 76

surmounting obstacles. The result is a waning of intense feeling in personal life (for which the increasing violence of public life may well be an unconsciously created compensation). If joys and sorrows have not much dignity and aims are usually self-regarding, life adds up to a small and boring total. Since everyone's mental life has probably taken in some of this spiritual pollution, elements of it may be traceable in the Christian's dryness and spiritual *ennui*. We may in fact be giving up too soon, because our understanding of what is involved in a journey of faith is too easy to be realistic and too dull to hold us.

Our generation seems, too, to be one that dare not show its ideals. Perhaps they are there, in some unacknowledged corner of the community's mind, but tacitly, because of a great nervousness about expressing them in words. So political discussion becomes a desiccated and cantankerous thing, without eloquence, but given to endless talk about money. In this enervating atmosphere there is no chance of an inspiration, such as might induce feelings of hope and compassion and long desire. Emotional life sags and hangs round the individual spirit, a crumpled flag around its staff on a windless day.

The church has not escaped this defeat of interest. People enter fully and responsibly into the realm of grace at confirmation, only to discover that confirmation is something you have and get over, like measles. Thereafter your longing for the infinite, for the splendour of the eternal light, is offered little more than ethics and fundraising. The let-down religious spirit looks round in exasperation and finds there is nowhere to turn unless to the way-out enthusiasm of the charismatic group or the exotic silences of transcendental meditation.

Ideals-starvation leads to a reduction of certainty about

traditional categories of right and wrong. Every new generation questions its predecessor's moral norms, and rightly. Their lack of experience is balanced by the fact that their looser position in the structure of social life enables them to entertain more objective appraisals and new sympathies. The process is quickened by the impact of certain new points of view. During the last hundred years western man has come to understand how personal behaviour is rightly, though not exclusively, to be referred to unconscious forces activated in early infancy and to social conditions. There is consequently considerable uncertainty about where blame is to be put, whether it is to be put anywhere, whether indeed it is a suitable word for an educated man to use. The rootless and restless are not confined to those who have consciously rejected traditional social norms but include countless kind people who feel they do not belong in their time and are for ever asking themselves questions they cannot answer, which accumulate in the mind and leave a great weight of undecided detail there. The tendency then is to withdraw into the small privacy of the self. It is not much to hold on to, and it is not particularly interesting, but it is at hand; so they cling to a set of purely personal interests, like limpets with their sensitive side stuck to a rock, while the sea of time rushes and tumbles and plunges past them so beautifully.

It could be argued that this too stable, inward-looking self is something the Church's teachers and leaders have conscientiously, sometimes courageously, fought against during the last twenty-five years. They have repeatedly urged the ordinary Christian to return to the world outside himself and the Church and become involved in its local affairs and national anxieties. There are several fine reasons for doing that, and they motivate many fine people; but the Christian is apt to feel cheated if he hears only the moral tune in the life of the Church.

The characteristic Christian reason for becoming mixed up in the world's need and its chaos is that God is there, that Christ has identified with the least of its frustrated and humiliated millions. And God's presence is the power to persist and be brave there in social action, as it is the patience to cope with one's refractory self, as it is the rightness of a perfectly calculated rest in a Beethoven string quartet. Part of the dryness of our time is the drying-up of that stream of sacramental teaching and practice that throughout the Church's history does seem to have been the most effective carrier of the presence, the holy, the grace of a world bigger than this. Religious people are certainly no better than others; but they want to see God, they want to know what that want and its satisfaction can possibly mean for them; they are ready then to have a look at goodness. God is indeed the only interesting thing in religion. He is why they came in.

One rather odd reason for dryness is that the satisfactions of faith may themselves mean its death. There are many impulses at work when we feel the urge to find an acceptable vision of reality and allow it a regulating place in our lives. Among them are the desire for meaning and coherence, the wish to make some headway with the obvious mystery, perhaps the sheer interest of some forms of spiritual life, the sense of death, of insecurity, the way this world can look so good and then suddenly seem as flimsy as paper.

Sometimes the Christian faith does so much to pull together these unorganized elements of one's mind that one comes into a new vigour and competence. Life is much more manageable; it actually begins to go well. And yet, mysteriously, or so it seems to the unwary, there is now less spiritual need. Your improved performance takes the edge off the appetite for the things of God, and you begin to find religion just a little boring.

The same process has a sinister role in marriage. Two lovers may find that the first ten years of being together satisfy many of their needs, marvellously. Together they negotiate certain challenges in their adaptation to one another and to the reality of the world outside their love, and they are stronger personalities for this success. And then one day they look round and realize that they no longer need each other quite as they did in the early days. The battles they fought and won then are now in their past, along with the insecurities that drew them together as beloved allies. Unless they discover a deeper range of mutual interest and need, and a fresh, contemporary liking brightens their loving, they are bound to feel their happiness begin to shake.

Religious faith must similarly wilt unless new bonds are continually made between oneself and God, so that one's spiritual life is a matter of present meanings and resists time's tendency to suck things back into the past. Many students find, five years after they have gone down, that the intense religious life of the student group is hardly recognizable as theirs, for they have no need of it now, no need of that specific range of prayer and gifts of grace. Life has moved on and made all that marvel something that cannot be even a grateful memory, only an anachronism. We have to keep pace with reality:

We must be still and still moving
Into another intensity
For a further union, a deeper communion.[4]

[4] T. S. Eliot, *East Coker: The Complete Poems and Plays of T. S. Eliot*, Faber 1969, p. 183

However, the call to move forward has sometimes an extremely unwelcome sound, particularly in times of depression. Indeed, for making faith seem not so much a way of life, more an arid programme, depression is definitely the thing.

The people who know this condition and its dreadful features, the barren heart, the parched mind, the seeking and never finding even a glimmer of light, are not exceptional by any means; much less are they exceptionally weak, in a spiritual or moral sense. Most of them have coped with their stint of life's problems, and been normally courageous and efficient, but have just met their match in what is facing them now. As a matter of fact, really severe depression is commoner than many people realize. It has been estimated that one person in four reaches a state of pathological anxiety at least once in his lifetime.

It is not the bewildering fatigue and the low spirits that form the most distressing aspect of it. It is the unpleasant mixture of self-reproach and unidentified fear, the waking early with a sense of doom of almost hallucinatory vividness, and the way one's mind is quite impervious to rational discussion.

It is sometimes argued that the severer form of this malaise is primarily to be related to an inner source, to some modification of the chemistry of the system. Another view is that there is just one disturbance, with a great variety of presenting signs, whose more serious manifestations stimulate certain chemical changes which themselves intensify it. Whatever the truth of that, there are some features and stages of depression which bring it into the realm of illness. In that situation it is obviously God's will that we seek his healing power as it is expressed in medical help. There is no doubt an abuse of the results of pharmacological advance in our time, but there is also a pride and a pseudo-spiritual highmindedness behind the refusal to submit one's trouble to medical treatment.

Much tension and sadness are not of this dramatic kind. The cause is generally some frustration, disappointment, humiliation or loss in the immediately preceding week or so. This experience of life's negative side is made more difficult to manage because it provokes resentment to a degree we are not prepared to acknowledge; and so an uncomfortable conflict situation is added to the original pain. The only way through is by self-understanding, the work of identifying the source of the current dismay or fear, and 'spiritual direction', both such as you give yourself in meditation and the sort you may receive from someone else who is skilled in this kind of affection.

I have to say that I find in myself a considerable resistance to this exercise, important as it is. One just does not want to examine one's gloom and trace the upset to its source in the hinterland of one's emotional experience. It is partly because our laziness shrinks from the work involved. At a deeper level there is the fear that when we see any of our angers and dreads clearly it will be obvious that we need to make changes in our attitudes. And that is apt to make us panic, because some of our attitudes have served us very well in the past in keeping us reasonably stable. At this stage there is no way out, there is only the way further in, in companionship with the enlightening and healing spirit of God.

It seems to me that the Christian way of living life is a journey in faith in two senses. We go forward in the faith that all experience is in one way or another an encounter with love as the Church has taught that huge idea, exploring that particular understanding of the human condition, making our own appropriation of it, discovering what in 'the faith' has life and meaning for the sort of people we happen to be, in different situations and at different times in our lives. But there is also the more emotional thing, the look and feel of life when you actually live it in Christian terms. One is a journey in understanding, the other is a journey in feeling; and both are journeys in that there is movement and progress, losing the way and finding once again that you know more or less where you are.

So, if each experience is a deal with love, then this actual wretchedness of depression is what it feels like just now to have God in *my* life. I may think that it is blotting out his presence, but it is in fact the carrier of it. It is the means of his coming. His presence is always truth and power for loving life, however obscurely, and however long it takes to realize this. Accordingly, the first thing to pray for is the grace to be hospitable to the formidable gloom because in it there is coming to me some vision of how to be merciful to life and find it after all a holy thing that I could not receive in any other way.

There is a famous icon by Rublev in which these deep considerations seem very much at home. It is known as *The Trinity*, sometimes as '*The Hospitality*'. The Father, the Son and the Holy Spirit are seated together in mysterious love round a table on whose white cloth a chalice stands. They look like angelic beings, their golden wings overlap as though they are old friends with their arms about each other's shoulders. They are shown turned to one another with an understanding look, content to let something pass unquestioned because a deeper truth holds them in its peace. Behind them is an oak tree, which is a way of saying that behind their silence and serenity is the Old Testament story of the visit of three strangers to Abraham. He welcomed them, though completely ignorant of their intentions and uncertain whether to be pleased or afraid. They were in fact infinitely more than friend or foe, they were really God, coming to confirm his promise to give Abraham a future of fulfilment and dignity. This profound imagery of welcome and suffering and God's disguise and the fulfilment of life makes Rublev's icon a steadying thing to look at prayerfully at any time but particularly in time of incapacity.

Everyone, whether disposed to see life in religious terms or not, needs to have some means of steadying himself and being still. The spirit of the times opposes such intelligent provision. It is a restless spirit, perhaps compensating in hyperactivity for the hopelessness and meaninglessness it glimpses when occasionally its gaze turns inward. That is hardly fair. If there is a deficiency of hope and meaning in one's being it deserves to be stayed with and considered; it is not fair to take one look and run. Many refuse to be still with themselves because they dislike what they are. So what? Don't we all? And we are all much harder on ourselves than God is. It is better to accept and wait and show some interest in your self and its needs and to believe that God's promise of a future for you is still good.

There is a place simply for doing nothing but waiting in faith. The faith is that if you do nothing (being furious with oneself is in fact doing a great deal) there is an inner wisdom in virtue of which your mind rights itself if you avoid struggling with it. The odds are that your struggles are applying quite the wrong pressures anyway. Surprisingly enough many people find, when they emerge from the inexplicable deadness, that simply by accepting and waiting they have moved on without being able to say how.

It would be ungrateful not to mention the help that comes through other people's ideas. It is not always easy to say why they should help; and sometimes you disconcertingly find that you are alone in seeing useful perceptions in some passage from a favourite writer. The power of the thing is often closely related to the language in which the thought is expressed. A thought about God can radiate light in one version of the Bible and be quite dead in another, though the meaning is the same. I have always liked the following examples of one human being comforting another.

The first is a fine and genuinely invigorating expression of stoicism.[5] Voltaire, at seventy years of age, wrote to his old friend, Madame du Deffand, who had written him a sad letter about her infirmities. She was old, no longer enjoyed life, and she was going blind. It is a long letter in which he sympathizes deeply with her, sharing much of her unhappiness, and then he launches into what he suggests as a remedy:

> It is not in your power or mine to save you from losing your eyesight, or to prevent us from being deprived of our friends, or—in short—from being in the situation in which we actually are. All our deprivations, all our feelings, all our ideas are necessary things. You could not help writing me the very philosophical and very sad letters which I have received from you; and I must, of necessity, write to tell you that courage, resignation to the laws of nature, a deep contempt for all superstitions, the noble pleasure of feeling oneself to be of a different nature from that of fools, the exercise of the thinking faculty—that all these are genuine consolations. This idea, which I was fated to point out to you, will necessarily recall your own philosophy; so that I play the part of one instrument that strengthens another—another by which I myself will be strengthened in turn. Happy the machines that can afford each other mutual support! Your own machine is one of the best in the world. Is it not true that if you were to choose between seeing and

[5] Voltaire's Correspondence (ed. Besterman), vol LV, no. 11045, tr. Jean Seznec

thinking, you would prefer the eyes of the mind to the eyes of the body? Come on, Madam, courage! Let us drag our chains to the last. *Allons, Madame, courage. Trainons notre lien jusqu'au bout.*

The second example is Sydney Smith counselling Lady Georgiana Morpeth on how to deal with melancholy:

. . . Nobody has suffered more from low spirits than I have done—so I feel for you. 1st. Live as well as you dare. 2nd. Go into the shower-bath with a small quantity of water at a temperature low enough to give you a slight sensation of cold, 75 or 80 degrees. 3rd. Amusing books. 4th. Short views of human life—not further than dinner or tea. 5th. Be as busy as you can. 6th. See as much as you can of those friends that respect and like you. 7th. And of those acquaintances who amuse you. 8th. Make no secret of low spirits to your friends, but talk of them freely—they are always worse for dignified concealment. 9th. Attend to the effects tea and coffee produce upon you. 10th. Compare your lot with that of other people. 11th. Don't expect too much from human life—a sorry business at the best. 12th. Avoid poetry, dramatic representations (except comedy), music, serious novels, melancholy sentimental people, and everything likely to excite feeling or emotion not ending in active benevolence. 13th. *Do good*, and endeavour to please everybody of every degree. 14th. Be as much as you can in the open air without fatigue. 15th. Make the room where you commonly sit, gay and pleasant. 16th. Struggle by little and little against idleness. 17th. Don't be too severe upon yourself, or underrate yourself, but do yourself justice. 18th. Keep good blazing fires. 19th. Be firm and constant in the exercise of rational religion.

It is remarkable how little one wants to alter (though there is just a little) in that advice of over a hundred and fifty years ago.[6]

[6] Quoted in David Cecil, *Library Looking-Glass*, Constable 1976, p. 249

My third example is from a letter by Henry James to comfort Miss Grace Norton in a time of suffering. He wrote it in 1883. He was a great letter writer and this is one of his greatest and a fine expression of his spiritual stance. It is a pity that one should make any cuts in it:

My dear Grace,

Before the sufferings of others I am always utterly powerless, and your letter reveals such depths of suffering that I hardly know what to say. . . . I don't know *why* we live—the gift of life comes to us from I don't know what source or for what purpose; but I believe we can go on living for the reason that (always of course up to a certain point) life is the most valuable thing we know anything about, and it is therefore presumptively a great mistake to surrender it while there is any yet left in the cup. In other words, consciousness is an illimitable power, and though at times it may seem to be all consciousness of misery, yet in the way it propagates itself from wave to wave, so that we never cease to feel, and though at moments we appear to, try to, pray to, there is something that holds one in one's place, makes it a standpoint in the universe which it is probably good not to forsake. . . . Remember that every life is a special problem which is not yours but another's, and content yourself with the terrible algebra of your own. Don't melt too much into the universe, but be as solid and dense and fixed as you can. We all live together, and those of us who love and know, live so most. We help each other—even unconsciously, each in our own effort, we lighten the effort of others, we contribute to the sum of success, make it possible for others to live. Sorrow comes in great waves—no one can know that better than you—but it rolls over us; and though it may almost smother us it leaves us on the spot, and we know that if it is strong we are stronger, inasmuch as it passes and we remain. It wears us, uses us, but we wear it and use it in return; and it is blind, whereas we after a manner see. . . . Don't think, don't feel, any more than you can help, don't conclude or decide—don't do anything but *wait*. Everything will pass, and serenity and *accepted* mysteries and disillusionments,

and the tenderness of a few good people, and new opportunities and, in a word, ever so much of life will remain. You
will do all sorts of things yet, and I will help you. The only
thing is not to *melt* in the meanwhile . . . so that however
fast the horse may run away there will when he pulls up, be a
somewhat agitated but perfectly identical G.N. left in the
saddle. Try not to be ill—that is all; for in that there is failure.
You are marked out for success, and you must not fail. You
have my tenderest affection and all my confidence.

Ever your faithful friend,
Henry James[7]

---

[7] *The Letters of Henry James*, ed. P. Lubbock, 1920, vol. 1, pp. 100–2

V

Masculine, Feminine and the Spiritual

ONE remarkable feature of the religious scene, or rather that part of it which is visible as the life of the Church, is that it appeals more to women than to men. In Judaism and Islam this is not so clear and indeed there seem to be signs of almost a masculine monopoly, though of course that can only be an impression that I have gathered from very inadequate reading. In western Christianity the high percentage of women in the congregation is obvious to everyone, though surprisingly enough its significance has not yet been considered with any thoroughness.

Generalizing about male and female characteristics is an unsatisfactory procedure because the problem is there in the words we are actually using. Many people are now uneasy with traditional stereotyping of men and women; they are less confident than previous generations that they can give a clear differentiation to the words 'male' and 'female'.

An obvious place to begin is the fact that in every society and culture it is women and only women who bear children; in every society the person closest to the infant and young child is a woman, so that the person with whom the child first identifies is a woman, and both female and male children have to mature by differentiating themselves from a woman, not a man. The basic process of the transmission of life, which provides more and more powerful images to stir and content the mind than any other aspect of existence, involves woman, her body, her caring and nurturing self, to an infinitely greater depth than it can ever involve man.

To which source is surely to be traced her readiness to respond to certain human experiences—those connected with birth, growth, love, marriage, the family, all that helps or threatens or destroys in these fascinating realms, and death that never stops hovering and sooner or later descends to kill. It has been remarked that both women and men know that it takes nine months to make a man and less than a second to destroy him, but women know it with a greater concern. It is out of human response to these experiences and the enjoyment and fear they spread through life that religion grows. Perhaps because of its deep root women more easily see the place of religion in life. They recognize that, however inadequately it does it, it is trying to be articulate about areas of feeling with which they are familiar.

I suspect that the general attitude of men to emotion plays an important part in their religious hesitations. It is a commonplace that men are dominantly turned towards the outer world. There are several signs of this, other than the obvious one of their traditional role as 'breadwinners' (which in any case is currently undergoing modification). The greater proportion of the prison population is male, the greater proportion of psychiatric hospital patients is female. When the male psyche is disturbed it acts out this disturbance in anti-social behaviour in the world. When the female psyche is disturbed, by some centripetal force it turns inward into one or other of the many forms of anxiety. If men's nature has this centrifugal tendency, it may well involve an inclination to alienation from the inner world of the self, its more elusive feelings and deeper wants.

With Englishmen, that alienation is reinforced by certain idiosyncrasies of national character. The idealized image of himself that an Englishman, absorbs simply by growing up in an English environment is on the whole a tough conception. It is a compound of many ingredients which include various forms of the idea of the strong man in our tradition, such as the stoic, the puritan, the empire-builder. Somewhere in it is to be found a stiff upper lip; its firmness is traceable in the old public school ideal, the mystique of scouting (as Baden-Powell originally conceived it), the Olympian imperturbability described in Kipling's poem 'If' (which even such an aesthete and intellectual as Sir Maurice Bowra considered as good a basis as any for a serious man's *examen de conscience*), and in recent times in the complex taste for violence, and the values, such as they are, of the world of violence. The power of this image of male toughness does not diminish much even though it is increasingly acknowledged that women have a longer life-expectancy than men, are not so delicate physically, and do not so easily collapse under bereavement and certain other normal human hardships and strains.

This ideal of toughness and courage results in a corresponding, if often unconscious, repression of the tender emotions, what has been called 'the taboo on tenderness'. It intensifies the natural masculine alienation from emotional depths and increases men's tendency to withdraw from those activities which involve the uncertainty and misty danger of the emotions. So they become ill at ease in the world of religion, the arts, the expression of one's not so easily identifed fears and dreams. The average Englishman's attitude to artists and poets is that incomprehension that easily moves into mockery and contempt.

If you live in a cultural atmosphere in which there is this

taboo on emotion you may be persuaded into operating with only part of yourself. No one is at his best, at his maximum, so operating. It is a situation likely to provoke feelings of inferiority. Another is that provided by the fact that men live in two worlds, the world of work and the world of home. Their work self is different from their home self, sometimes much more fulfilled, sometimes a burden they are intensely relieved to drop as they start for home at the end of the day. If you change yourself with your suit you may begin to have doubts about your selfhood, though the process may well be a subconscious one. Even so, when they come home men assume a self that is not necessarily equipped for this domestic role. In English education there is practically nothing to prepare a boy for his future role as husband and father.

Such considerations may suggest a consequent male insecurity. The standard defence which the insecure ego puts up in its unconscious panic has a number of well-known forms. One is the arbitrary assertion of rightness, the opposite of the feeling of failure. This easily operates as a kind of allergy to all authority, to being told what one should do, to having the realm of personal inadequacy opened up. This must inevitably make men allergic to religion. I am sure that one of the reasons for the many jokes about parsons, apart from the fact that we often give the impression of being not part of life but at a kind of tangent to it, is that the parson represents the world of religious and moral authority. Men are restive in that world. Laughing at it, in the person of the clergyman, is one of the ways of hitting out at it. This hostility to religion is sometimes fed by the presence in the unconscious of a harsh father-image, the fear and resentment it generates being projected on to God the Father. The converse could well apply in the feminine inner world where it is the mother-image that so often provokes unease, while God the Father, or Jesus, stimulates a positive response, being in a sense her first lover.

The sexual and religious dimensions overlap in various ways. I have the impression that because women are more at ease about their sexual nature than men are this aspect of religion does not create any problems. Men are less integrated sexually, maybe more guilty, and are embarrassed and suspicious over signs of the merging of the religious and the sexual (for example, in erotic imagery in some hymns).

I am sure that the mental climate of the twentieth century is inimical to such stirrings as quicken the masculine religious self. I have never had reason to think that English people are deeply religious by nature, or even given to the aspirations of idealism. Their response to life is pragmatic, they feel that what matters is practical life, indeed they are preternaturally moralistic; what matters is how you behave, and creeds, doctrines, sacraments, church-going are thought to be remote from 'real life' and in any case do not seem to have made much difference to those who bother with them.

This phlegmatic and pedestrian disposition is set in an aggressive civilization that is continually overstating. The world of advertisement, the mass media, political campaigning and trade union pressure, in some respects the world of religion too, take to overstatement and exaggeration like ducks to water. You cannot fool all the people all the time. In the end your efforts are counterproductive, or else they produce a kind of 'punch-drunk' situation in which people find it difficult to be excited about anything except football. In Richard Hoggart's analysis of the 'common man' he says:

He is infinitely cagey; he puts up so powerful a silent resistance that it can threaten to become a spiritual death, a
creeping paralysis of the moral will. . . . Outside the personal life (people) will believe almost nothing consciously;
the springs of assent have nearly dried up. Or worse they
will believe in the reducing and destroying things but not in
assertions of positive worth. . . . As a reinforcement there
is, behind, the disinclination to strike attitudes, to take
oneself too seriously, the slowness to moral indignation, and
in addition, the 'Leave me alone. Ah'm as good as you' cry of
the disappointed decent man.[1]

Those words were written twenty years ago but they
seem to me to refer just as accurately to the current
situation. It is one of tiredness, indiscriminate scepticism
and rejection of most of the great words that have spoken
for the splendour and the tragedy that dignify the fate of
man. Englishmen naturally find it hard to believe deeply
and must find it harder in today's climate.

Moralism tends to operate against religion not only in
the obvious way, by being a substitute, but also by raising
critical problems. Many men have a quite vivid appreciation of the deep challenge presented in Christianity to
the hold we ordinarily have on material things, pleasures
of the senses, the world of amusement. They feel that they
could not take Christianity seriously without a radical
loosening of this dependence, and they see clearly that
they are not prepared to re-orientate themselves in this
way. So they must stay outside. I was once trying to
explain to such a man that I saw 'Go, sell that thou hast
and give to the poor' as God's word to one particular man
and that it is not to be expected that he will say it to every
man, though everyone realizes with something of a
tremor that one day that may indeed be God's word to

---

[1] Richard Hoggart, *The Uses of Literacy*, Penguin Books 1959, pp. 232–3

him. My friend thought that a typically clerical and unnecessary refinement, lessening the immediacy of the command's relevance.

As a matter of fact it is an issue which leads further into Jesus' religion than most of us have time to go. The words of Jesus are marvellous for taking you into the heart of a problem, where divine grace and human limitation face each other, and showing you you have got it wrong if you think life is an affair of question and answer. It must always be, at the important levels, an affair of tension. Useful things can be said about the forces pulling you in half, but to escape from them is not on, not unless you are willing to miss much of life's interest.

The refusal to take Jesus' religion seriously because the things he asks for are so startling is often just perfectionism. The choice is not between accepting (however sadly) a corrupt and selfish world and opting for some purity of love and simplicity to be created, if at all, only by those who have dropped out of the sinful mess of the twentieth century. The choice is between moral indifference and recognizing that love is alive and well, doing a lot to change conditions so that it can have more room, and calling for a bit of help.

Another perfectionist is the anxious type who will not undertake, or withdraws from, activity in which he may not be an outstanding success. Within that superficially respectable gesture there lurks a self-concern that unconsciously requires one impressive performance after another to bolster its shaking confidence. There may also be an unrealistic resistance to the mere idea of spiritual effort because the fear of failure makes us unwilling to have a go. However, Christianity says some good things about failure, because we are never going to be anything else and it is directed with a special mercy to this feature of the human condition. Normally Jesus presented his view of life's prospects as a joyful thing, bringing relief and fulfilment to people depressed by failure of one kind or another. When we have begun to enter into his view of things and the way of life that goes with it we find that God asks this and that from us; but it is as we can bear it, and in any case he is the giver of what he asks. There is no such thing as the challenge of the gospel without the grace of the gospel, without the offered strength and forgiveness and the persisting appeal of the way of Jesus. He gives us the courage to continue trying to love, which he seemed to identify by its truthfulness and its tenderness. He had an extraordinary gift for spotting humbug, but always without pride. He trusted his vision, and translated it into clear and spare ideas, spoken with wit and epigrammatic flair, so that they stick in your mind like burrs on your clothes after a country walk.

When men succeed in breaking through the many barriers on the way to faith and arrive where the way opens out into Jesus' world of light they are, of course, intensely religious—so much so that as a sex they have dominated the development and spread of Christianity.

All Christian dogmatic theology has been written by men. Women such as St Teresa of Avila and Mother Julian of Norwich have had an important place in the realm of mystical theology, and they have figured repeatedly in the drama of Christian martyrdom; but it cannot be denied that theology, ecclesiology and the main tradition of Christian spirituality are the creation of men. There have been historical and cultural reasons for this masculine dominance in the past, but they are rapidly ceasing to be cogent, and a new situation emerges in which women can redress this imbalance in theology and spirituality.

I am not able to say what I expect from such development, only that I suspect that the feminine contribution to spirituality has hardly begun. It is often observed in the protestant tradition that at any rate there seems to be little difference between the preaching of men and women. My view is that that is to the impoverishment of the ministry of the word and due to the fact that homiletic instruction and the preaching models are all male.

Naturally one would not expect this great division of humanity into two sexes to be notably present in highly technical and cerebral situations like a discussion in higher mathematics where presumably the participants are reduced almost to being functions of their intellects; but in any utterance that concerns the existential depths of the self one would expect it to be evident. What meaning people are able to affirm in life's joy and pain, what appals them, what in any human situation assails their attention most quickly and compellingly and makes them want to cheer or groan, surely when such experience is put into words women are going to speak differently from men. The difference will not always be vast; it will range from considerable difference in point of view to the merest nuance. Both utterances are needed if men and women are to find the truth.

This need is one of the implications of the Bible's idea of creation, that that which is made in God's image must therefore be a duality. 'So God created man in his own image . . . male and female he created them.' If the likeness of God is to appear on earth one sex cannot carry it. Only by men and women knowing, understanding, loving one another can it be known what God is like, and only by coming to know God can men and women fully know what it is like to be a man or woman.

The idea that there is mental masculinity and femininity

is not easy to elaborate. I think that if one did not know, one could tell that the writings of St Teresa, Virginia Woolf, Elizabeth Bowen, are by women, but that if one did not know to the contrary one would assume that *Wuthering Heights* had been written by a man. Certainly there seems little that is feminine in the writings of Simone Weil. It goes without saying that, whatever masculinity and femininity are, they will appear in different proportions in individual men and women. Not only is it the case that 'male and female he created them' but that, to add to the fascination of it all, male and female he created him, and her, planting the duality deep within the individuality of each.

Virginia Woolf saw a marvellous androgynous balance in Shakespeare, and in Keats, Sterne, Lamb and Coleridge, a 'little too much' of the feminine in Proust, and a preponderance of the male in Milton, Wordsworth and Tolstoy, while neither Kipling nor Galsworthy had even 'a spark of the woman in him'.[2] Her view about Tolstoy surprises me. It seems clear that to women *Anna Karenina* is the work of a man who, when the preacher in him stopped thundering, understood them. On the other hand, for another example, there is little evidence that women think that D. H. Lawrence travelled far from masculine assumptions, though that is not to deny his great stature as a writer.

An attempt to detect these elements in spirituality was made some years ago by Dr Valerie Goldstein. One of her ideas is that male personal development from birth to maturity is more anxiety-provoking than female maturation, and particularly that it is characterized by an on-going need for personal justification, a consequent difficulty in entering into relationships in which self-

[2] Virginia Woolf, *A Room of One's Own*, Penguin Books 1945, pp. 84–6

concern is at a minimum, and a continual need to have his maleness as it were under-written. He requires 'a kind of objective achievement and a greater degree of self-differentiation and self-development than are required of woman *as* woman. In a sense, masculinity is an endless process of *becoming*, while in femininity the emphasis is on *being*.'[3]

On this analysis the masculine mind would seem to be inclined to preoccupation with anxiety, guilt and self-justification. Anxiety, guilt and justification are certainly notable features in Pauline theology. That is not to knock St Paul. Let him remain in all his glory—and it is glory—but let the suggestion also be considered that he sounds like a very masculine male and analysed the human predicament and the Christian revelation from an honestly masculine standpoint. It can then be suggested that this is perhaps just half the truth and that we need the riches of Christ and the hunger of the human spirit described with similar intensity and intellectual power by a woman.

Before that can happen it must be truly and extensively wanted. It is of course useless for women to write and speak about God self-consciously as women. Any adoption of a role, any wish to plead their fifty per cent interest in humanity's spiritual quest, can only make their expression of their religious self untrue. It must come from their openness to their own inner and outer experience, their own realization of how joyful it is to be alive and how chaotic and disillusioning, their discovery of what they really want from God if indeed what they want from him is something they care to consider. What God means

[3] V. S. Goldstein, 'The Human Situation, A Feminine Viewpoint', *The Nature of Man in Theological and Psychological Perspective*, ed. S. Doninger, Harper 1966

97

to woman man can only know as she tells him, as she gives him to drink from her well of truth, because he has nothing to draw with there and the well is deep. In his turn he must be honest and clear about what he finds in his journey of faith. Together they may come to some wholeness in their thought of God and life and love.

The complementary character of their experience, for the sphere of love, has been well suggested by Alan Ecclestone[4] when he pleads that the recognition of sexuality's place in spirituality, and a happier welcome to all of this tremendous dimension of human experience, will make for a much more informed and imaginative understanding of marriage. 'There is a great balance of injustice, hatred, blindness and cruel insensitiveness to redress and make reparation for on behalf of women. There is equally great need to rescue men from a fearful legacy of self-hatred and tormented distrust of sexuality which has maimed and so often robbed them of their opportunities to grow through sexual relations to greater maturity of living.' He deplores a long tradition of 'what looks like a-sexual spirituality' and argues that we are at a stage where 'prayer itself must search unweariedly for a new and authentic Yes, where men and women together must speak to each other with an honesty and openness for which there are no precedents to appeal to'.

And in the journey of faith itself men and women need the same awareness of each other's full legitimacy in the knowledge of God and the same desire to know what the other both knows and wishes to know of the Spirit. And they must try to get as much of it into words as can in fact be so expressed. It is a difficult exercise. There is however general agreement today that we are suffering from an

---

[4] Alan Ecclestone, *Yes to God*, Darton Longman and Todd 1975, pp. 91, 96

extremely sharp need for freshness in religious communication, for men and women of inner strength and independence who will feed on the good in the great tradition, reject the obsolete and the facile, and then forget both and be utterly themselves before God and life. When that happens, what they say about God will be certain to be interesting.

This might well result in a more imaginative, because less unisex, spiritual direction. Christian teaching has usually interpreted sin in terms of self-assertion, will-to-power, and the using of people as things rather than meeting them as persons. That interpretation is certainly relevant in the masculine world, with its innate need for self-justification and the anxieties relative to the aggressive, the ambitious, the competitive character. However, the feminine journey to God does not appear to go through that kind of psychological country; and the spiritual direction that assumes that it does is likely to achieve something less than illumination.

Pride and selfishness, as commonly understood, are not the distinctive weakness of women to which you may expect them to be reduced on the difficult day. Woman has a characteristic capacity for the opposite posture, for surrendering her individual concerns in order to meet the requirements of others, in the first place the needs of her child and then those of her husband and others. The more plausible suggestion is that feminine weakness is in part precisely along the line of unselfishness and its exaggerations. The thought of being a person on one's own account, a real, interesting, eternal thing, whose needs, integrity, privacy, quiet, development all require understanding and care—this exciting and productive thought many women will not allow themselves to entertain, considering it an indulgence; and men have certainly not discouraged them in this repression. It results in an unreadiness to recognize and cope with the secret hostility that is always concealed in human loving when it is completely other-orientated, and an anxiety that is unnecessarily guilty about the tight interdependencies of affection and exasperation in relationships.

While generalization comes too easily in what is after all a highly emotive subject, there are some landmarks for a rough map of male and female differentiation. Most analyses describe man as the more independent and adventurous, and more likely to see the world in terms of things and ideas; and woman, because of her nurturant role, as the more affiliative and stable, and more likely to construe the world in personal terms and register its moral and aesthetic values. These contrasts indicate the probable exaggerations of our endowments, the direction in which each of us, losing hold, will unconsciously drift. So, women will veer towards being over-conscientious, dependent on others for confidence, liable to triviality and indiscrimination, insufficiently objective; and men towards being manipulative, able to dispense with people, insensitive to subtleties of fear and grievance in others, liable to obstinacy, narrowness and the theoretical approach. Each sex has its own God-given capacity for good and consequently its own closely related capacity for evil. Indeed there is a classical view that regards evil as the result of a good impulse operating unreasonably. The power of reason in us, such as it rather hesitantly is, is continually challenged by influences from our personal history and current environmental conditions. None of us is entirely masculine or entirely feminine. In each of us these sets of characteristics are mixed in varying proportions. But it is as composites of that which is man and that which is woman that we make our response to God and experience our deviations from and approximations to a mature and happy life in Christ.

All attempts to see these matters a little more clearly should return for inspiration to the Bible, to its awareness of the mystery both of what separates and what unites male and female. 'So the Lord God caused a deep sleep to fall upon the man, and while he slept he took one of his ribs and closed up its place with flesh. And the rib which the Lord God had taken from the man he made into a woman and brought her to the man. Then the man said "This at last is bone of my bone and flesh of my flesh".'

The association of the creation of woman with man's sleep is intriguing. Sleep is the realm of the dream. Dreaming is a product of man's unconscious life, its deep seated longings and confusions. Figures in dreams are usually of multiple meaning and reference; they carry associations with the immediate and the distant past in enigmatic complication. So the passage can be construed as a way of saying that the knowledge men and women have of each other has something of a dreamlike quality. Profound, not always recognizable wants and fears operate mysteriously in it. For example, in man's mind there are often unconscious fusings of the image of his mother and that of his wife, in woman's mind similarly unconscious blendings of the image of her father and that of her husband. Some of the pain and difficulty of loving can be traced to this mix-up of dream and reality, to the way memory and fantasy complicate things as men and women try to be truthful and kind to one another.

And Adam said 'This at last is bone of my bone and flesh of my flesh'. That is to say, she is made of the same essential stuff as he. However much men and women differ, become estranged, are a mystery and a puzzle to one another, drift into conflict—nevertheless, they are two of a kind, they belong. Fundamentally they cannot help wanting and fearing the same things. Their essential human longings and dreads will be expressed differently often. There will be a masculine form of the need for security and a feminine form of it, and this will involve each in different hopes and expectations of the other, and of God. Still, the ties that bind them are so many that they stand together, over against a whole universe that cannot produce even one of their most casual thoughts and feelings. One flesh and blood, both of them dread being left alone with their humiliations and failures, neither can manage an excess of hurt, each must go to someone, somewhere, for protection if life threatens to overwhelm, and both are made for love.

VI

Mother of God

TO understand anyone at all you need to be on his spiritual wavelength. With Jesus, this requires the exercise of a highly trained and sensitive historical sympathy. The world in which he awoke each morning and went to sleep at night or stared into the darkness, the thoughts and feelings that made these human repetitions his own, are so remote from us that loving him must include learning how to sustain this discontinuity.

It is the tremendous ministry of the scholars (as it seems to me, never sufficiently appreciated in the Church) to help us. Their work involves both placing him in the past and rescuing him from the past for us. They can help only so far, the difficulties facing them being so great and our ability to follow them being so limited. If the ideal of 'faith seeking understanding' means just seeking to understand Jesus as research seeks to understand the life and writings of Shakespeare, Christianity would be of interest mainly to antiquarians. That classical ideal of faith, however, means that one seeks to understand God and life, and that it is through Jesus Christ that one does this; and Jesus is not a body of literature, however sacred; he is now a religious world, of almost indefinite width and depth, in which people come to God, go from him, return and are received again, and have been doing this for centuries.

In spite of the difficulties, we cannot stop wanting to know Jesus, this mysterious figure, occupied in bringing people hope or despair as their individual need apparently was, sometimes peremptory, sometimes so generous you would think that this tough world contained no heart hard enough to resist him. He was not afraid to come down to our level and admit his need of comfort, yet we find him drifting from us in his peculiar view of life as locked in a fantastic conflict and his sense of time running out for us all. The gospels assemble a few fragments of a life and leave us to put them together to make a man. Very few people are shown bringing him any good news, most came showing him how for them in one way or another life had got out of hand. People went to him, apparently, when they were in trouble or when they were frightened; and the troubled wanted to use him and the frightened wanted to be angry with him. Most human actions have manipulation or aggression in them somewhere; the thing is to get some other properties into them, like affection and joy.

And all the time he is doing this religious thing, pointing people to God, without rhetoric, always with acceptance of the facts, using paradox and suggestion but little exhortation, and most of the time in his own heart shaken by an extraordinary sense of being hunted by death. He exposed himself without thinking, almost naturally, to death, fortified by the one attitude that can cope with any experience, however awful, that God is the kind of love that will see us through, if we want him with all of us that is at our command.

Sometimes one wonders why one should bother to read anything but Jesus. Certainly the trade in Jesuses is as brisk as ever, in scholarship, in popular writing and in television. It is always interesting to see what others make of him and his words. All seem to love him and to want to find some positive relation between his interpretation of

life and the lives they are living. No one wants to dismiss
him. Many people feel that their happiness is some kind of
blessing and even forgiveness and so suggests the rightness of gratitude, and at the same time they sense the
strangeness of life as though there is another life more
human than this, that we would find more natural, of
which we catch occasional glimpses; that is to say, they
sense that there is an unseen world and that many of our
experiences, perhaps all, are transactions with it. And no
one has spoken so importantly to this mood as Jesus. Yet
when we respond to him we begin to divide; we feel the
edge of the sword which he said (with some grief) he
realized he had brought; and it turns out that the vision of
Christ one man sees is often the enemy of another man's
vision of him.

It is this hugeness and fascination of Jesus that has
oddly enough made me think of his mother and see a
mystery about her too. I say 'oddly enough' because I
have learned Christianity in a tradition in which devotion
to the mother of our Lord does not exist, though you
never know what goes on in people's minds. I am quite
sure that far more of our people think about her than are
able to acknowledge it. Anyway, a time came in my own
journey of faith when I found my imagination repeatedly
drawn to her, as it still is. I had sensed long ago that, if
Jesus is what the Church says he is, she must matter. Then
as my understanding of Christianity expanded I found
that the great majority of Christian believers know that
she matters, have known since the second century, indeed
since the first, because the infancy narratives are dated as
first-century material and are (as I understand them) not
so much history as a paean of praise to God and her for
him. Since then there has poured through the life of the
Church a fantastic flood of praise for her on the slender

thread of whose existence hung so much of the world's joy and meaning. I want to think about her intelligently. I mean that I want to be able to justify what I think about her. I am aware that it is easy to make her a composite figure, indulgent and compensatory, carrying more of one's hungry self than truth; but it is equally easy to do that with God. I want to avoid that if I can, with both God and her.

The name of Jesus has become a great concentration of meaning as the Church has packed so much experience into it. The mind cannot take it all in at once and naturally attends to this or that part of the whole, not as detached from it but as a symbol and focus through which the whole reality that is Jesus becomes accessible. The Blessed Virgin Mary is part of his world and a focus of its meaning. The first person who ever loved him, she carries and represents the praise of all who have since felt certain that he is the light and warmth of our life, and their oneness as a family, and the mutual care that is the family's life-blood. Khomiakov said: 'The blood of the Church is prayer one for the other and her breath is praise of the Lord.' Devotion to the Mother of Jesus is another way of appreciating that.

It is a pity that such devotion is not well supplied with congenial forms of prayer, but that is not an unfamiliar situation in the prayer of the Church. The few congenial forms come deep into the life of the Church, into the endless repetition that is the Church at prayer; the rest, in their feebleness and inadequacy, wander round the Christian family, perhaps achieving a modest and brief popularity, but eventually fade away homeless and unreceived. I share the general affection for the Angelus, the Rosary, the Salve Regina, and I am grateful for a few of the Marian prayers of Orthodoxy, but like many others I have spent too long hunting for congenial prayers of any kind and conclude now that vocal prayer is one of the realms in which a little is enough and that in this very difficulty silence is summoning us to take the all it can give. It does seem that Marian devotion has found its most satisfying expression not in formal prayer but in art, in the building of the great cathedrals and innumerable churches, in much painting and sculpture, and in such an outpouring of heavenly music that must often have stopped evil in its headlong course.

Occasionally I come across a poem that marvellously gives life to her image in the mind, as does Gerard Manley Hopkins' poem 'The Blessed Virgin compared to the air we breathe', and certain poems by Rilke and Edwin Muir. Sometimes a part of a poem not written about her may strike me as saying well what may be said about her. This happens with some of the poems of Wallace Stevens (for example, 'To the one of fictive music') and even, strangely enough, of Baudelaire. Actually there is nothing strange about it at all. She is a world of meaning. It is the work of the inspired imagination to bring together different worlds of meaning in momentary harmony. And this so effectively brings to a focus 'the various impulses of the self, so as to suspend them in a single image, that a great peace falls upon that perturbed kingdom'.[1]

The poet and artist, David Jones, who died in 1974, has a long, and in parts extremely obscure, poem called 'The Tutelar of the Place' which makes much of the idea of the Blessed Virgin Mary as the great archetype of the individual and concerned about the individual, in contrast with the ruthlessly general and mechanistic character of twentieth-century life:

[1] George Santayana, *The Sense of Beauty*, p. 235

. . . mother of particular perfections
queen of otherness
mistress of assymetry
patroness of things counter, parti, pied, several
protectress of things known and handled
help of things familiar and small
wardress of the secret crevices
of things wrapped and hidden . . .
receive our prayers

. . . sweet Jill of the demarcations
arc of differences
tower of individuation
queen of the minivers
laughing in the mantle of variety . . .

when the technicians manipulate the dead limbs of
our culture as though it yet had life, have
mercy on us.[2]

Of course, you have to accept the way your religious self functions. I know nothing about the vivid personal presence of which some people have spoken when describing the place of the Virgin Mary in their religious experience. And generally speaking I have never been able to find much reality in highly personalized religious images of the warm and intimate kind you find, say, in Charles Wesley's hymns. I find myself disinclined to invoke Jesus by name, except in the Jesus prayer—but there it is the invocation of a name not a representation of a person; and certainly I have never had any vision or feeling of God as present in a personal manner and would not have the faintest idea what to do with it if it came. So, the mother of our Lord is not for me an unseen accompanying presence, but she is so frequently in my

[2] David Jones, *The Sleeping Lord*, Faber 1974, pp. 62–4

thoughts, links together so much devotion and life, is associated so profoundly with intercessory love that I can never now think her away from the Christian religion. Yet there is nothing narrow and obsessional about this. It just happens to be the case that one does not want to rest indulgently in any thought traceable to her alone. What she is leads one to think of the communion of saints, and Christ himself, and the word of God, and that blessedness is in hearing and keeping that word as it is daily signified.

T. S. Eliot once said that prose is the language of ideals, while poetry is the language of reality. It is an idea that surprises people and makes them think at first that it is the wrong way round, that surely prose deals with reality, poetry with ideals. However, if you stay with it you see the kind of truth it has. Prose, using logical procedures as traditionally understood, is the appropriate vehicle for coming to a conclusion, making a practical recommendation, finding a solution to a problem. Poetry is the kind of language in which a whole situation is presented and its feeling communicated, so that you know what it means to see a certain segment of reality with your whole feeling self, to contemplate a person or an object sympathetically enough for it to exercise its full force upon you. Pages of prose could be written to set out what Blake's poem 'The Sick Rose' is about, but, however full such treatment might be, something, indeed the all-important thing, eludes that procedure. You can find the poem real, and presumably share something at any rate of the experience of the poet, only by living encounter. You have simply to read the poem and you will come face to face with it.

It seems to me that some, at any rate, of traditional Christian thought about the Blessed Virgin Mary has this character of being the vehicle of reality. The doctrines of the immaculate conception, the virgin birth, and the assumption, are part of the radiance shed in the mind of the Church by that blaze of light which is the incarnation. They communicate certain realities which do not otherwise strike the imagination so powerfully, realities like the awe and wonder of the incarnation and the fact of its origin in God. Something like that is what the virgin birth imagery is 'saying'. It is not asserting a biological freak as evidence of God's saving presence in the world; it is an attempt to convey that in the life of Jesus of Nazareth, his isolation, his lovableness, his all-round gaze, his power to terrify and to give hope, it is God who is amongst us. In order that we may fully realize it, that it is God's truth and love, we need something more than to be told it prosaically. We need it carried into our beings much more deeply than intellectually, by imagery that is rich in echoes of the past and sets up a resonance throughout our whole self.

The poet W. B. Yeats said once that he believed in what he called 'unity of being'.[3] His father had taught him the term, arguing that beauty, when truly apprehended, does engage the whole of us. If a musical instrument is properly strung, when one string is touched all the others murmur faintly. Similarly, there is not more (or less) desire in lust than in true love, but in true love there are other effects as well; for in true love desire awakens pity, hope, affection, admiration, and, given the right circumstances, every emotion possible. And when that total excitation happens it becomes clear that something more than this one person is being loved; life is being loved, and God himself.

I am sure that religion has to make plenty of room for this language of reality, in Eliot's sense, for what he calls

[3] W. B. Yeats, *Penguin Critical Anthologies*, ed. W. H. Pritchard, pp. 82, 83

poetry. Christian worship and private prayer need to be almost entirely expressed in it in so far as they are verbal because in them it is the whole self that is responding to the spiritual and it wishes to be as completely engaged as possible. Religion must of course try to explain itself. For its own sake as well as for its debate with the world it must try to say clearly as much as can be said of what it means and intends; but it cannot all be decoded or translated into logical discourse of the technical kind, it can never become simply information. Some of the liturgical revision of recent years, the *New English Bible*, and most of the contemporary forms of worship have this in common—they are interesting and marvellously forgettable. They cannot suggest, they do not produce religious life within us that goes on after they have stopped. Their atmosphere of pedestrian instant-comprehension means that what is subtle and complex in the life of faith tends to slip through their large mesh. Much that is religion can be expressed only indirectly. This is why there are some features of the meaning of Jesus that make their impact only through devotion to his mother and the thoughts and feelings associated with her in the Christian imagination.

One of these thoughts that are given summary form in her is the idea of the oneness of love. The mother of Jesus is often called (to the embarrassment of the unimaginative) the Mother of God. Her love for her son is one and the same as her love for her God. She becomes in prayer the place where it is said that all human loving reaches its fulfilment as it becomes the love of God, as it becomes loving God.

That does not mean that by some pious mental gymnastics we have always to see only the Creator in the creature. A mother, in one of love's primordial contentments, gazing at her two-month-old baby after he has been fed, is not supposed to pull herself together and think of God, as though she has nearly fallen into idolatry. God does not wish to be substituted for her son, to take the place of her son in her affection. God's will at that moment is that she love her little human son. God has placed himself, as the object of her love, in the form of her child. It is a kind of incarnation. It would be an idolatry only if her loving stopped there, at her child, if her child was all she really loved.

All human loving reaches its fulfilment as it becomes loving God. Our loving others will be more truly loving them, instead of using, possessing, dominating them, as it is ordered by our love of God. The Christian faith is that, as we grow in our loving, our love of the world and our love of God will blend. In heaven we shall love things and people and God in one single love, as the Blessed Virgin Mary loved God and her son in one love.

We approach this the more loving we do. The wider and more varied our loving is the more it will be protected from the deceptions and narrowness which must make love a so much weaker thing. It has been said that a woman can be a truly loving mother only if she can love beyond her child, only if she is able to love her husband, other children, strangers, and a multitude of things.[4] Otherwise she will perhaps hardly love even her child. She will be so dependent on this one relationship that it will be open to question who is being loved, and when she takes her crying child in her arms she may well be staring over his shoulder at her own loneliness.

When loving is so reduced, monopolized by one relationship, it cannot be at peace within, because jealousy is waiting there coiled in its heart, since it must be afraid of

[4] Erich Fromm, *The Art of Loving*, Allen and Unwin 1968, p. 42

being robbed. And sooner or later it must turn into hostility, as it grows disappointed that the love-object cannot sustain its role of being perfectly lovable. Any living thing cast for such a role must fail. We live in a time when love is often transformed into aggression under the pressure of fear and disappointment, and far too often meets with condemnation. The judgemental attitude merely compounds the aggression in a situation in which only understanding can save anything from so much pain.

It is true that the world's imagination is marvellously fired by certain examples of obsessional love. Hippolytus and Phaedra, Tristan and Isolde, Abelard and Héloise evoke our passionate response because of the well of romanticism in us and the dream of a tragic love soaring high over all life's conditions. They are also signs for love's fatality, its unplayable-with power. They are magnificent, but exceptions, in that they do not disclose the true character of love in its wholeness.

Loving is primarily not a relationship to certain people and things considered lovable, but a disposition of the whole self to life. The more widely we love, the more deeply we love; this is because we are in fact becoming more loving, we are able to put more love into each loving relationship. Our loving becomes more a function of the whole self, not of simply a bit of it. Christian faith proposes an ideal of always loving, at all times and all places, so that our love of our children, our desire to have some beauty in our life, our concern about life's wrongness and what we can do, are all one and the same love of the incarnate Lord.

Jesus has impressed generation after generation as being someone who loved in this mature way, with the whole of himself, so that even on the days when life was terrible he was fully there, and what he did with it was recognizably the response of love to it. He was never against it. That he achieved this undismayable goodwill, so that you could always trust him with life at its most tangled or intransigent, is part of the mystery that he is, but within that mystery, in her own light and grace, stands his mother. Everyone knows that our ability to love is connected, however obscurely, with the kind of love we received when too young to love. The kind that is truly creative is the love that stimulates and encourages the child's own loving, the most precious bit of his and anyone's humanity, so easily damaged in the early years that no one would dare to be a parent were it not such fun but, if it survives, strong enough to take any horror that life at its most malevolent can serve up. A mother cannot offer love like that unless she has an existence of her own, can give because she does not need to possess, can let go because she is delighted to see the authority of love appearing in another life.

Another way of putting this is to say that her child's first deep relationship is largely her work and it is the one he will later use as a model for others. Within that relationship her most crucial work is to enable him to tolerate without anxiety the test of not being in specific relationship, to bear separation from her for increasingly long periods. Otherwise he will become an internally lonely adult, indulging himself in this and that, clutching feverishly at chance acquaintances perhaps, not able to bear the standard human day. So the student, who was brilliant when supported in a peer group at school, begins to fail as he struggles to work alone at a university, unable to concentrate, devitalized by the empty flavour of being on his own. Not that this means that a good mother will give her child some unnatural strength. On the contrary, she must leave him his freedom and spontaneity to cry out for whatever help may be going when he cannot take any more of life.

It seems that all this the Blessed Virgin Mary gave to Jesus. He had had love, so he was able to love, to love and to need love in the openness and honesty of a mature heart. So we honour her who taught him the language of love, gave him his first image of it; we are profoundly stirred to see that when he comes fully into view at the beginning of his extraordinary vocation he has memories of her that never pulled him back in nostalgia for some lost paradise but inspired his freedom to go forward in God's purpose.

There is a very ancient tradition, which mystifies many people, which associates the idea of perpetual virginity with the mother of Jesus. It was formalized at a sixth-century Church council, but long before that it was part of the way Christians thought about her. We receive from the Christian past an image of our Lord's mother as having no natural children, as being a young widow, entering more and more deeply into the mystery of her life's meaning, and gradually transformed from the Mary of history into the Mary of the Church's love and prayer, where she remains to this day a radiant and tantalizing presence.

She comes with this strange title 'Ever-virgin'. It is not a definition in physiology, nor is it an item in a historical enquiry. To think of it in such ways is to mistake the language. It is an image in the 'language of reality'. It is of the imagination and communicates to the imagination, initially of women but ultimately of men as well.

As long ago as the fourth century they were arguing for it, people like St Ambrose and others; and what was being argued was in principle a view of woman as other and more than her fertility and sexual functions. She is a self.

She has an inalienable individuality and freedom that entitle her to her own privacy, to keep things in her heart and let its depths speak to her of fulfilment, the fulfilment God means her to have, whatever the world plans for her. The satisfaction she desires may owe nothing at all to what in any generation is expected of her or of life, but the essential thing is that it should be the outcome of her own choice that this or that deep thing is going to matter to her supremely from now on and for ever.

I understand that Gertrude Stein distinguished between a person who is an 'entity' and one who has an 'identity'.[5] 'Identity' is what society gives you—your role as parent, teacher, doctor, industrialist, parson, obliging society by your quota of service. So today, in some quarters it is said that priests and ministers have an 'identity-crisis' on hand, because they are not sure that society wants them. On the other hand, a person who is an 'entity' is a being, and is related to ultimate being and its freedom, which is a totally other dimension than the world of doing, and so is at liberty to dismiss the world's distractions, and for the time being its just demands as well, and can enjoy and suffer the dignity that comes of being just that. It is as though Christianity began to see and understand freedom not by looking at man's various powers of doing but at woman's absolutism of being. The title 'Ever-virgin' is the Church trying to find the first words for this absolute freedom of choice and commitment which Christ's coming enabled it to see in feminine nature.

It is certainly freedom to go against current evaluation of the feminine role, yet it implies no deviation from the essentially feminine. Being woman and mother is not to be defined exclusively in physical terms as being a sub-

[5] Cf. Saul Bellow, *Humboldt's Gift*, Penguin Books 1977, p. 304

missive link in the great chain of procreation and assuming a domestic role. That is in no way to denigrate physical sexuality and motherhood. It is simply to entertain a more comprehensive understanding of the word 'feminine'. It is all obvious to us now, though it certainly was not obvious to anyone when the Holy Spirit began teaching this to the world. To us now it is quite clear that to argue that women and men, in order to fulfil themselves, to reach their capacity, must have sexual and parental experience is to have got it all wrong. It means to have misunderstood life so much that one has joined the narrowing and dehumanizing influences that are making our society rot. It is failure to see the marvellous light round man's head, that he is made in the image of God. If he is indeed so made, then all the doors of his life are open, and whichever way he walks it is a straight road to infinity.

Man is the only creature that is made in the image of God. That is the characteristic that distinguishes him from the animal creation. Whatever it means it cannot mean the ability to join in that physical continuum that is the transmission of life. It must be a wider thing, quite beyond the grasp of all the evolutionary stages that have preceded us, though perhaps giving them meaning. It is in fact the ability to be a self, to be someone who thinks, plans, imagines, loves, and follows the call of the spirit whether the world cheers or laughs or just does not want to know.

To invoke the name of the Blessed Virgin Mary in prayer means to be in earnest about the line you have chosen on the perplexity of death. Our generation is not on good terms with the thought of death. What security it has (I mean the inner thing, peace of heart) is not as secure as it used to be. It depends too much on judicious reticences, on people trying not to notice what alarms them. Much of the old assurance about a life beyond has gone. Yet people still register the old protest against death; they find the face of mortality as unacceptable as ever. At times everyone catches himself considering alternative attitudes. Perhaps things do not end as the bitter gates open. No one can prove to me that I shall not see him, her, them again, that I have just got to live quietly and hopelessly on now. Indeed even to our generation, so inclined to gloom about these matters, the case of death's finality looks about as unmade as ever.

If extinction is all that we can expect, then it seems more or less right to take a very personal and changeable view of what matters in life; it makes sense to beware of becoming too serious about anything. The tantalizing thing is that we cannot settle with that. It does not feel right. We want to be real people, which must mean people who are open to reality; so that when pleasure or pain approaches, or some memory comes up from behind, or for some inner reason we begin thinking what on earth all the varied pain that human beings endure can possibly mean, we are ready for any of these alternatives, we can let it happen and do not have to distort it or soften its impact by some shaky defence mechanism we have adopted. If there is a range of experience that at all costs we cannot allow ourselves, it is probable that it will increase. One fear tends to lead to another. We shall be reduced to protecting our mental and emotional house from so much of the world's weather that our sheltered life will begin to bore us and then become a kind of suffocation and claustrophobia. We shall want to get out of it because it has begun to feel like death.

And perhaps that is death. What we actually call death may be another thing altogether, and much less lethal.

That becomes a stronger possibility when you think of the good that lights up human life and gives it dignity and when you consider the superfluous suffering that pulls it down again. There is nothing in our world to account fully for either, to explain the one and help us accept the other with no further questions to put to existence. They seem to require more room than space-time supplies for them to begin to make sense. If, however, there is a world of growth beyond this one, a satisfactory meaning for good and evil could well be there.

It is to that world of meaning which alone gives mortality an acceptable face that the Blessed Virgin Mary belongs. She does not represent its fulness and triumph as Christ does, but she is part of it. Her special significance in the Christian mind lies in the fact that she is one of us, as fully and only human as the rest of the cloud of witnesses, so that in principle every prayer invoking her name gives us once again the feel of death's feebleness and makes the beyond familiar since it is inhabited by men and women who are prayed for and loved.

That is too important a belief to leave just a belief, something you say in a creed on Sundays. To anyone who thinks it is true it is like the invigorating air of break of day. Devotion to the Mother of Jesus is one of the means of breathing this deeply thought happiness about our human future. She is one of the ways Christians talk about life and live it. Their idea is to use as much of it and reject as little of it as possible. To do that one needs a usable way of thinking about death, so that one can live intelligently in time, knowing its incomprehensible length and the quite obvious brevity of individual life, and draw sustenance from that, life from it, rather than fear and sadness. Christians do not think anything of that mournful refuge of the middle-aged—that death is far enough away still and there is plenty of time to think it all out. Most people never have the luck to find that store of time and draw on its mythical leisure. They discover simply that their perspectives change, they are no longer able to live by the old programme they have got used to, but they have no words for the deeper thoughts welling up from some obscure part of them they never knew they had. So they feel lost, like stateless persons, outside the frontier of their own life, only surviving by resolving to feel less, since emotion is too disturbing.

Especially those involved in the important enterprise of ageing, who have to give time now to organizing the deployment of energy and the maintenance of valid dignities—it seems all wrong that these should have, as well as arthritis, a stiffness of attitude to what has always appeared on the last horizon, and should have to turn so many thoughts away. By contrast, the relaxed and less agitated have a marvellously natural look, human and often amusing. Very near the end of her life, Rose Macaulay, feeling her age, wrote to her friend Sacheverel Sitwell: 'I'm thinking of pushing off this summer. I'm getting so vague. I wrote a letter to someone the other day starting off "Dear Sachie".'

The faith that the grave is not a dead end but a way through is often attacked on the grounds of its supposed comfort. The idea seems to be around that the truth is sad, as all intelligent people know, and brighter readings of life must be suspect. There could, however, be an unconscious wish behind that as well. Given suitable conditions, anything can be secretly wanted, even extinction, which can meet the longings of world-weariness just as satisfactorily as any sentimental heaven. Why should the exhausted assume that the terrestrial process is kind enough to give them all-concluding death? The wishful thinking with which Christians are charged by humanists can just as easily be reversed.

In any case it is not a question of comfort. The Christian Church does not argue much for the comfort in the idea of eternal life, though it is not disposed to put any premium on discomfort. The claim is that life has meaning, that eternal death is an unacceptable idea because it is the negation of meaning, and meaning implies rational consequence to human actions. A door then opens on to an infinity of possibility, both glorious and grave; but that is all in the meaning-package. Nicolas Berdyaev wrote of faith in eternal life as bringing into his life, along with many other ranges of meaning, a source of terror and responsibility. T. S. Eliot was thinking on similar lines when he wrote in a letter to a friend: 'I had far rather walk, as I do, in daily terror of eternity, than feel that this was only a children's game in which all the contestants would get equally worthless prizes in the end.'[6] That was written in 1930. Eliot came to know an assurance in which that daily terror was worked into and quite transformed by a less anxious faith. But Christians will always find it difficult to express in words their experience of human responsibility and divine mercy; they will certainly never manage it without the use of paradox and ambiguity and will always suspect that they have said either too much or too little.

The hope of eternal life, like all the Christian ideas about God, and the meaning of our birth and death, and what is worth doing to fill up the interval between the two, belongs to that kind of truth that is seen to be true only within the life of faith; and that means among the people of faith, their way of praying together in the presence of some bread and wine, and their daily, often ungainly, attempts at loving. It means feeling hurt by

[6] Quoted by B. A. Harries in *Theology*, vol. LXXV, Jan.-Dec. 1972, p. 142

what makes them suffer and encouraged by the unusual perspectives on human woe their scriptures give them.

The mother of Jesus was the very first Christ-lover to work through this slow, sometimes difficult, process of learning to believe. She came to know God first through the friends of God of her tradition, the old Israel. In this way she came to know God as a God who speaks, either directly or through certain moralists, poets and politicians whom she and they regarded as messengers of the truth. They taught her that God is a spiritual reality of infinite capacity, into whose hands it is both a dreadful thing and our salvation to fall, and that he has a unique purpose for each one of us whose realization is essential to everyone else's happiness. It is important, therefore, to learn how to wait in life's silence or noise, alert for any signs to us of what this purpose may be. She came to know God also in the glimpse of absolute joy every happy mother has, when her firstborn son was first in her arms.

As the years passed and she observed his growing sense of God and encouraged it, saw it taking him far beyond her understanding though not beyond her love and faith, she tried to think through the mystery of his being, in fellowship with his friends and in her own solitary reflections. She did this as a mother, in whose arms he once lay, a helpless minimum of human life, and once again, a helpless dead thing. And she did it as woman, whose being is naturally other-regarding, given to the concerns of efficient love, and at the same time is so constituted that she is continually drawn to look within, at herself and at something deeper, at what is as deep as God. A divided creature, in whom the dimensions of being and doing meet in mutual challenge and reciprocal aid, she seems at times made for God only and at times for life only, and her life is to make them not alternatives but one thing.

That is of course no more true of woman than of man, only certain times and certain conditions have made it and will make it more difficult for one than for the other.

So she and her friends went through all they had to go through in his company until he was so outrageously taken from them.

She came to know the risen Christ in the same way, as they did, as we all do, within the group who loved him, through all that happened to them and their efforts to understand it. The New Testament gives a vivid picture of this in its account of the first Easter weeks. Their minds are disturbed by something, someone, who comes, is recognized, surprisingly eludes, sometimes terrifies. The evidence accumulates, to become a presence who now unmistakably brings them peace, commands them, gives them a feeling of authority for his continuing work. They grope through all this, evaluating it as best they can, not too sure how much to believe. Finally they reach an astonishing joy, described in the Bible under images of a return to Jerusalem and the beginning of the work into which every Christian has been gladly or hesitantly drawn.

It soon became clear that it was not going to be always joy. Before long the work and the joy stopped being easy and became a matter of faith. It happens in human love as well as in religious commitment, which are in fact very much alike. Two who are fairly certain that love has installed its legendary self in their delighted hearts realize after a while that rather more effort is required. A stage may come when for a time they live entirely on trust, in the faith that the love that is there can survive whatever has happened, whatever may happen, to their very last day, because what has its arms around them may not be particularly good but is is certainly God.

No one in that first Christian group can have found this experience of love and faith, love into faith, more perplexing and eventually so tremendously happy as Jesus' mother. It was her heart that had been most pierced by the sword of his death; her heart must have been the most lifted up by his resurrection. In the same way it is Christian believers today, who languish in a truly religious grief because they feel surrounded by what seem so many signs of his death, who have most to gain from his appearing to them in another form. It is eminently worth their while to wait for this to happen, and deliberately to make certain mental clearings so that they are ready for it should it be in some outlandish form, like a mere man working in a garden, as indeed it once was.

There is every reason for persisting at this waiting and looking. There are always reports that someone has seen him, somewhere, somehow. So many people just now are having religious experiences of different kinds that research projects on the subject are proliferating like mushrooms in autumnal meadows. The looking has to be as open as possible, unrestricted enough for you to run the risk of being mistaken. A sympathetic image to keep in the mind is that of waiting on God, waiting for God, but a waiting so alert that what it waits for is almost there, and its arrival will not be a surprise but a recognition. 'The faith and the love and the hope are all in the waiting.'

It is a good condition to be in. Many people who say they have lost their faith are in the best possible state for appreciating this. Usually, all they have lost is a lot of secondhand mental furniture that they never much liked because it was never theirs. It was handed down to them by well-meaning parents and teachers or taken by them from conventional religious stores. It is good to throw that out and in true poverty of spirit set out on your own.

What you discover for yourself has an unmistakable reality and interest, though it needs to be taken into a sane religious tradition, to be related by critical comparisons and confirmations with other people's discoveries. Otherwise it can degenerate into eccentricity and superstition and nonsense, or else just vanish like something spilt on sand. That can happen both outside and inside the Church, though the risk is greater outside.

This journey of personal discovery is for everyone now. In the past it seems that people accepted as simply true the beliefs given them; and religion for them was principally their sharing in various rituals, that may well have spoken truth to their unconscious depths, and their acknowledgement of certain moral principles backed by the beliefs. It was only a minority who set out on a personal search. For them the rituals and the morals were necessary but subsidiary to this more intense and costly affair, the personal discoveries that were the material of what they really believed. That minority is now the majority, in the sense that if people today are going to have any religious belief it can only be as a genuine matter of personal urgency.

So nearly all are looking, waiting on life and God, in hope. When I pray for all of us who share the warmth of the sun and the more thought-provoking sight of the stars, it is that we shall not miss any of the meaning of our experiences, especially those when life takes on a specially meaningful look and the spirit receives the sudden shock or excitement or even amusement that marks its encounter with truth.

The mother of Jesus has had many titles given her, because she has had so many significant roles in the Christian imagination. Somewhere, sometime she must have been called 'Our Lady of Faith', though I have not discovered that this is so. It is a view of her that is congenial and natural. She had to make her own journey of faith in the risen Christ, of faith in the resurrection of life. It was the same journey that we have to make, a journey of understanding and experience, an exploration of the reality of God and of the possibilities of life there are in all sorts of death. She made it, as we do, among the friends of Jesus, after his dreadful fall from their happy world, as she continually asked herself if this and that and some other thing could by some stretch of imagination be regarded as his presence, as the presence of God. Growing older, she found she could answer 'Yes' to that question more often than not, sometimes timidly of course, though sometimes with delight, because in all losses he was never lost, was indeed with her always, to make of her acceptance and faith a new song to replace the one she used to have in her heart.